Horse Showing for Kids

Horse Showing for Kids

Everything a young rider needs to know to prepare, train, and compete in English or Western events. **Plus:** getting-ready checklists and show diary pages.

Cheryl Kimball

WITHDRAWN

**The mission of Storey Publishing is to serve our customers
by publishing practical information that encourages personal
independence in harmony with the environment.**

Edited by Deborah Burns
Art direction by Lisa Clark
Cover design by Wendy Palitz and Kathy Herlihy-Paoli
Front Cover photographs © Gemma Giannini, left; © Shelley Heatley, right
Back Cover photograph © Shelley Heatley
Cover illustrations © Jean Abernethy
See page 148 for photography credits
Color illustrations © Jean Abernethy
Pencil illustrations by JoAnna Rissanen
Text design by Carol Jessop
Text production by Jennifer Jepson Smith
Indexed by Robert and Cynthia Swanson

Chart on page 98 © 2003, Suzanne Drnec,
    Hobby Horse Clothing Co., Inc., used by permission

Printed in China by Elegance
10 9 8 7 6 5 4 3 2 1

Library of Congress Cataloging-in-Publication Data

Kimball, Cheryl.
  Horse showing for kids / Cheryl Kimball.
     v. cm.
  Includes bibliographical references and index.
  Contents: Types of shows — Types of classes — Show personnel — Choosing
the right horse — Conditioning and training — Trailering — Grooming — Attire
— Planning for a show — On the big day — After the show — Moving up the
competitive ladder.
  ISBN 1-58017-573-2 (alk. paper) — ISBN 1-58017-501-5 (pbk. : alk. paper)
  1. Horse shows—Handbooks, manuals, etc.—Juvenile literature. 2.
Horsemanship—Handbooks, manuals, etc.—Juvenile literature. [1. Horse
shows—Handbooks, manuals, etc. 2. Horsemanship—Handbooks, manuals, etc.]
I. Title.
  SF294.7.K56 2004
  798.2'4—dc22
                                        2003021732

Acknowledgments

I would like to thank the following judges, instructors,
and competitors, who had so much information to offer,
I could have talked with them each a lot longer.

Carla Wennberg
Cindi Adams
Pat Thompson
Joanne Gelinas Snow
Stephanie Levy
Lowell Murray

And, of course, I thank everyone at Storey Publishing,
a great group of people to work with; in particular
Deborah Burns, an editor full of patience and encouragement.

Contents

Good luck to you!

How exciting that you are interested in the world of equestrian competition. To be competitive while keeping the best interests of your horse in mind is a balancing act. If you do it well, you will be amply rewarded — sometimes with ribbons, sometimes just with your horse's appreciation!

To compete in the horse world means a lot of hard work. You will often be thrilled with your progress and at other times you'll be discouraged. That's okay! Those times when you think that you and your horse will never get it together can be the ones where you learn the most.

There are a few important things to know about showing horses — some rules to follow and some etiquette to keep in mind. This book will guide you through all of these aspects of showing horses. You will also learn about taking care of your horse under the stress of competition. And you'll get some tips on keeping yourself in a winning frame of mind.

This book also emphasizes safety. As you probably already know, horses under any circumstances can be dangerous animals, just from their huge size and weight! Add the excitement and energy of the horse show environment and there's a lot to think about. You and your horse will be prepared if you follow good safety tips at all times.

So, are you ready to ride?

— *Cheryl Kimball*

PART 1

All About Showing

ONE

Different Types of
Horse Shows

If you own a horse or ride regularly, someday you may want to compete in a horse show. Showing has many wonderful benefits. Like a test in school, it forces you to prepare, practice, and polish. Setting goals and working toward them will improve your skills and strengthen your partnership with your horse. At the show you will meet and learn from others who share your interests. And at the end of the day, you have a judge's objective opinion about your and your horse's skills and training.

The first step is to decide what you like best to do with your horse. You can find a competition for almost any kind of horse activity you enjoy.

You Gotta Believe!

"The thing that makes me more comfortable in the show ring is to believe in my horse. My horses give me all the confidence I need. It doesn't matter what your horse is; he doesn't have to be 'world class' or expensive. If you believe in your horse, you will show with confidence. He needs to be world class in your eyes."

– Pat Thompson,
veteran showmanship and halter competitor

Pleasure Shows

The most common horse show is one that combines many different kinds of riding and has separate classes for each. These are called **pleasure shows.** The different classes in a pleasure show demonstrate how enjoyable your horse is to ride. In the same show, you can enter:

◆ a **pleasure** class, where you walk, trot, and canter around the ring

◆ a **showmanship** class, where you demonstrate your handling skills by leading your horse through a ground pattern

◆ a **trail** class, where you and your horse negotiate obstacles like opening a gate and walking over a tarp

◆ a **working hunter** class, where you show your horse over jumps

Pleasure shows often divide into classes designed for young children, teenagers, and adults. They will also break down into Western, English, or open (see page 5). Sometimes pleas-ure shows have one or two other kinds of classes mixed in, like jumping or barrel racing. And some breed-specific pleasure shows will have several open classes that other breeds and all levels of riders can enter together. Pleasure shows are the logical place to start your show career.

Pleasure shows are the most common type of equestrian competition.

Gymkhanas

A **gymkhana** is a program of mounted games for individuals or teams. If you and your horse like running around barrels and poles and other fast games, this is the perfect kind of show for you.

Gymkhana classes are usually timed, with very specific rules about whether and when you can trot or canter. You trot or canter around the poles and barrels in a specified direction. Whenever a class in a show requires that you ride in a specific pattern, the pattern is posted early in the day. In chapter two of this book, you will find some tips on how to memorize a pattern. Be sure to know the pattern *before* you mount and warm up your horse.

Open Shows

"Open" means that any breed of horse can enter, and exhibitors do not have to be members of the association that is sponsoring the show. In open classes, anything goes: English, Western, novice, and youth all compete against one another.

A gymkhana (pronounced "jim-KAH-nah") is a program of mounted games, fun on your own or with a team.

Show Story

Jennifer and Rex had been competing in pleasure shows for four years. They started out in Western classes, but Jennifer took a couple of English lessons and decided she liked it. After a winter of lessons, she switched to English pleasure classes, occasionally taking Rex in a Western pleasure class just to mix things up a little.

But then the English pleasure classes got boring. She found herself apologizing to Rex before they went in the ring, and she found herself thinking about everything but showing as she went round and round and round, walk, trot, canter, turn around, walk, trot, canter, line up, back up, the winner is . . . over and over and over. If she didn't change something, Jennifer thought someday she would go right to sleep up there and fall off Rex into a mud puddle, still snoring from the boredom.

But she liked competition. So she started to check around and see what other kinds of shows she might like. And that's when she discovered jumping. She knew she could compete in several types of jumping shows: over fences in the pleasure show ring, an environment she knew well; stadium jumping, where the whole show consisted of jumping and you jumped in the arena over fancy fences; and cross-country jumping, where you flew through the woods launching your horse over logs and stone walls. That's what she aspired to, cross-country. She could also do three-phase eventing, which combined stadium jumping, dressage, and cross-country.

Now Jennifer felt pretty revved up about her show career. She knew Rex was probably not the horse to take her far on the cross-country jumping path. That was okay, though: Her little sister, Lena, was starting to show some interest in showing and Rex could babysit her while Jen searched for just the right horse. Now things were feeling exciting again!

Performance Shows

A number of performance organizations sponsor shows in which horses of all breeds compete in specific activities. Examples are dressage, three-day eventing, and hunter-jumper. These shows can take you to the highest level, where the competition is international and intense (and the entry fees are higher!). Many performance shows feature Youth classes.

Dressage

Dressage shows are quite different from other types of shows. Each rider competes alone in the ring in what is called a **test.** Tests are given at different levels: Pre-elementary, Elementary, Beginner Novice, Novice, and Training are for the horse or rider new to dressage. As you and your horse learn, you move into the Intermediate levels toward Grand Prix, the highest level, where only the top riders and horses compete. Because dressage is such a painstaking discipline, you should expect it to take many years to reach the upper levels of competition.

You must sign up for a dressage show ahead of time. A couple of days before the show, you either call the show manager, receive a postcard in the mail, or check a Web site telling the time of your test. You need to be at the show, tacked up and warmed up, in time to enter the dressage ring at the exact time of your test. A judge sitting at one end of the arena scores your test.

If you want to be a great competitor, however, you will arrive early enough — and stay long enough —

Dressage riders compete individually in tests of their own skill, not in classes.

to watch some of the other riders compete. Observe competitors not only at your own level but also at the higher levels, where someday you intend to compete yourself.

Hunter-Jumper

Some shows are nothing but jumping. But there are two types of jumping, which are judged very differently.

The "hunt seat" style of riding originated with the foxhunt, where horse and rider encounter uneven terrain and natural jump obstacles such as stone walls and downed trees. Stirrup length tends to be short to help the seat come out of the saddle for two-point jumping position and galloping. "Working hunter" classes at shows reflect this history.

The "show jumper" focuses mainly on an arena course, jumping within a time limit and receiving penalties, called **faults,** for rail knockdowns, refusals, and going overtime. The course is usually about 15 jumps. Ties result in jump-offs until a winner emerges.

One phase of the Three-Day Event is the "cross-country" competition. The ultimate goal for a Three-Day Eventer is to ride on the U.S. Equestrian Team, like Karen O'Connor (above).

Three-Day Events

Three-Day (also called Three-Phase) Events are a true test of horsemanship. On separate days, you compete in a different discipline: dressage, stadium jumping (jumping in the arena), and cross-country (jumping out in the woods and fields). Eventing is exciting and takes a lot of hard work and preparation. It is a real test for you and your horse to compete in such a variety of activities and environments. As with any discipline, some horses are better at eventing than others. Above all, you and your horse will need lots of stamina.

Breed Shows

If your horse or pony is registered, your breed association will probably have a whole set of shows just for you. For instance, the American Quarter Horse Association sponsors shows around the country that are open only to registered American Quarter Horses. Arabians also have a well-organized national breed association, as well as state affiliates that sponsor regional shows.

By the Breed
In a breed-specific show, horses of the same breed perform in many different disciplines. A registered Paint horse might compete in a variety of classes.

Show jumping

Reining

Costume

Dressage

Within a breed show, you can compete in a variety of classes such as those described in the next chapter. It can be fun to compare your special horse with others of the same breed. Sometimes big general shows have classes designed for specific breeds, and you can sign up for those as well as open classes.

Some shows are even specific to a horse's coloring. Pintos, palominos, and buckskins have separate associations in which horses of a particular color can be registered. Many of these "color breeds" have their own shows. Your horse can be any breed, as long as he is the right color.

Miniature horses have become very popular over the past few years, and some clubs have mini classes in their pleasure shows. If a club has enough members with miniature horses, it might hold separate shows just for the minis. In general, if your horse is a specific breed and you feel that there are enough members with that breed in your club, you might explore creating some special classes.

Pick Your Show!

As you can see, there is no end to the types of shows or competitions you can enter. Your choice will depend on your personal interest, or sometimes it depends on your horse or pony: If he is a specific breed, you might choose breed shows. You might fall in love with a particular discipline, such as jumping or dressage. If you and your horse work hard, you can try several different disciplines before deciding which one is best for you.

A **circuit** is a series of shows put on by a specific association in a region. You earn points by competing and placing in a variety of shows. If you accumulate enough points in the shows in a particular circuit, you are eligible for year-end awards. You should go to all the shows in the circuit and enter several classes in your division (such as amateur or Youth) at each show to acquire enough points to become Grand Champion or Reserve Champion in your division.

Whatever you choose for your show season, be prepared for a lot of hard work and a lot of fun!

Secrets of Success

You will learn some tricks of the trade that will help you best show your horse to the judge. Some things you just have to learn as you show. But here are some age-old tips:

◆ **Ride into the ring ready to show.** Although the class doesn't officially start until everyone is in the ring and "Class closed" or a similar announcement is made, you are making an impression on the judge the moment you ride into the ring.

◆ **Know where the judge is!** This may seem obvious, but if you don't know where the judge is standing, you can't make sure the judge sees you at your best and doesn't see you at your worst. And it is always good form to avoid nearly mowing down the judge. This may sound funny, but it happens at almost every show.

◆ **If you know the judge is look-ing** at you, ride for all you're worth! In a big class, you won't have many chances to know the judge is watching your performance. Don't show off, just be as smooth as you can possibly be.

◆ **If you know that one of your horse's gaits** is better than another, try to stand out from the crowd during the good gait and blend into the crowd during the bad gait. To be a winner, the judge will want to have seen you move at all gaits, but if you are lucky, the judge will be looking in your direction when your horse is moving nicely.

◆ **Except when you are trying** to blend in to hide a bad gait or side, for the most part stay out in the open away from others. Invariably, no matter how big the arena, riders tend to clump up together. If you can pass one horse to get into an open space, fine. Otherwise, cut across the ring if you can do so smoothly without having to veer off to avoid the judge or the ring steward or anyone else.

◆ **When you pass** or try to move to an open space, do so in the gait that the class is currently in. If everyone is trotting, don't rush to the open space at a canter!

◆ **Always pass to the left** of the rider in front of you when you are coming from behind and always pass left to left when you are passing in opposite directions.

Profile:
U.S. Equestrian Federation

If you plan to have a long horse show career, you should become familiar with the United States Equestrian Federation (formerly called the USA Equestrian and American Horse Show Association). Also known simply as "the Federation," USEF's goal is to provide leadership in equestrian sports in the United States, "from grass roots to the Olympic Games."

USEF rates almost 3,000 shows in the United States each year. Although many USEF competitions feature English riding, they also offer Western classes like reining, as well as driving classes and events. These shows have strict rules and various divisions, such as Amateur and Professional. When you become a member, request a copy of its rule book (see the resource list on page 148 for the address).

The rules for serious competition are complex. An adult, trainer, or lesson barn that has been involved with USEF events for a long time can help you keep things straight and make sure you get off to a good start. For example, you might not be aware that two officials must measure your pony at your first qualifying show and you must receive a height card before you can compete.

USEF keeps track of your points throughout the season. If you want to accumulate points, ride in the same classes in all the shows you attend. You can check on your point status on its Web site, or join and receive e-mails with results of USEF-sanctioned events.

Where to Find Out About Shows

If you want to show in your region, subscribe to a regional horse publication. Regional magazines usually put out a huge calendar section in March or April and update the schedule in each month's issue.

Your local show barn will also know where the shows are and may itself sponsor a regional (or even national) show. And if you live near a university that has an equestrian program, it will sponsor a show or two in the course of the show season.

Of course, the ultimate place to look for information is online, and finding horse shows is no exception. For instance, if you look on the U.S. Equestrian Federation Web site, you will find a "competition search" entry that allows you to search the entire United States for shows by entering a zip code, discipline, or city. The listing also includes contact information so you can find out anything you need to know that isn't provided on the site.

Using a Coach

If you are new to horse showing, you might make better progress with a coach. This may or may not be your riding instructor or your horse's trainer. You may take regular riding lessons, but your instructor may not be in a position to be your show coach (for example, she may be just an equitation instructor). Your horse's trainer may be a great trainer but is not into showing. Someone has to show you the ropes. A good coach has years of show experience herself and is able to teach others patiently. Your coach should:

◆ have a personality that suits yours;

◆ not work with too many students, so she can give you as much attention as you need;

◆ be knowledgeable about the latest trends in showing style;

◆ attend your first few shows (if not all of them) with you until you learn the ins and outs of showing.

A coach could be your regular riding instructor or someone who works for your lesson barn. She could be your 4-H leader or the college student from down the street who used to show every season.

Of course, you will need to pay this person. How much depends on how much time she spends helping you. You can keep the cost of a coach down by using someone who coaches a group of riders. Ask around for the going rate for coaches in your area, and talk to your friends and other competitors about their experiences and any recommendations.

Your coach, whether she is a trainer or a riding instructor, should be someone who makes you feel good about your riding. Learn to avoid negativism and you will have a happy show career!

A coach is a trainer who specializes in preparing riders and horses for competition.

Ask Yourself

Showing horses is a big commitment. Training for your horse, lessons for you, practice, tack, clothes, transportation, and entry fees all add up to a lot of time and quite a bit of money no matter how carefully you budget.

How do you know you really want to show your horse? If you are feeling pretty lukewarm about it, like maybe you'd just as soon clean your room or something equally boring, or if you just don't feel quite ready for the show ring, sit this one out and gear up for the next. You'll know when you are ready. If you aren't sure, sometimes you just have to give it a try.

Here are some questions you can ask yourself to help you decide. Write your answers on the lines below or photocopy these pages and use them with your friends or fellow club members.

Do you love to compete?

Do you get very serious even when playing a game of Candy Land with your youngest cousin? If so, you have a competitive spirit and the thrill of showing horses might be just right for you! If you are not especially competitive and don't mind your little cousin always winning Candy Land, don't worry; you can still enjoy horse showing. Sometimes just seeing how polished you and your horse can become and participating in the social atmosphere of the horse show environment is enough. *Write how you feel about competition on the lines below.*

_____

_____

_____

_____

_____

Once you decide to do something, are you good about practicing?

In order to compete in a show, find out what you need to do and then practice it. With your horse, of course! It's not fair to your horse to go to the show without having practiced your classes. You don't need to spend hours drilling – that's not fair to your horse either – but you should put in a little time almost every day. *Fill in the lines below with your practice plan.*

_____

_____

_____

_____

_____

_____

_____

_____

Do you enjoy being in the limelight?

Even if you don't, that shouldn't keep you away from showing. There are lots of classes where you can blend in with the rest of the competitors. But you don't want to blend in too much; after all, you want the judge to notice you! Even if you are a little performance shy, there are ways to become more confident. (See chapter 10.) Once you have competed a few times, you will be less nervous. If you have anxiety attacks before a performance, you may want to avoid the dressage ring for a while. But don't forget, even there you aren't alone – you have your trusty mount right there with you. *Describe how you feel about performing, on the lines below.*

_____

_____

_____

_____

_____

_____

_____

TWO

Different Types of Classes

There is a lot to learn about horse shows and all the different classes that are available. It's a good idea to try some different classes before deciding which you like the best. If you really want to do one kind of riding (say, pleasure classes only) but all your friends are into jumping, don't be afraid to focus on what you like best. But don't be afraid to try something new, either!

In this chapter you'll find more detailed descriptions of the classes in a show, along with some things to think about when entering them. First, however, a word about judging.

It's All Relative

"It is important to recognize that your results at any horse show have as much to do with what your COMPETITION did as it does with what YOU did. Regardless of where, or if, you placed in a class, you (and your trainer or coach) must also be sure to evaluate each performance in comparison with your earlier efforts. Often you will find 'unsuccessful' days — in the competitive sense — can prove to be the most valuable when it comes to learning and advancing your level of skill."

– Linda Allen, *judge and international hunter-jumper course designer*

Two Ways of Judging

There are two different types of classes: those that are judged objectively and those that are judged subjectively. What's the difference?

Classes that are judged objectively, like show jumping or gymkhana classes, have a time limit or a series of obstacles that determines your success. Usually, one rider performs at a time and is judged on certain criteria: For example, you either jump a fence cleanly or knock down a rail. Your round is usually timed: If you exceed the time limit, you lose points for every fraction of a minute over the set time. The horse/rider combo with the fewest points, or "faults," wins.

Classes that are judged subjectively depend on the professional judgment of the judge. Specific criteria (such as time and faults) are not part of the class. In a pleasure class, for example, the riders compete in a group to respond to the judge's instruction, such as "Trot!" or "Line up!" Whichever rider does the best job according to the judge wins the class. (It's rare, but the judge can choose not to award first place if she doesn't think anyone deserves it!)

Unlike show jumping, hunter-jumper classes are judged subjectively, on "performance, manners, way of going, and style of jumping," says the United States Equestrian Federation (USEF) rulebook.

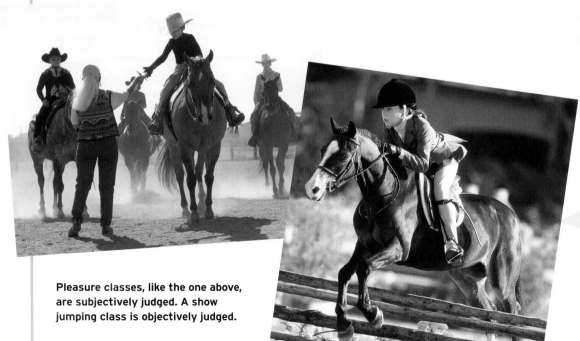

Pleasure classes, like the one above, are subjectively judged. A show jumping class is objectively judged.

Leading vs. Riding

The phrase *in hand* means that the horse is being led. *Under saddle* means you are riding him. Halter and showmanship classes are shown in hand.

Halter

Halter classes are based on the horse's conformation rather than his (or your) abilities. You lead your horse into the ring without tack. You may be asked to trot your horse for the judge, or sometimes you just have to stand in the center. Your goal is to put your horse's best side forward, both in appearance and in behavior. Your horse will be compared to other horses in the class who are the same breed and/or same age, and usually the same sex — mare or gelding. (Not many youths have the experience to show a stallion.)

◯ How to Catch the Judge's Eye

Since halter classes are judged on appearance, your horse must be fit, healthy, and impeccably groomed. Find out the latest style of grooming for your breed: Should the mane be left natural? Clipped? Braided? If it doesn't matter, do whatever becomes your horse the most. If she has a nice neck, braid her mane to show it off. If her neck isn't her best quality, keep

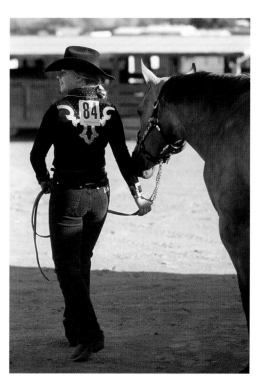

A halter class judges your horse's conformation and appearance. A showmanship class (see next page) judges how well you show your horse "in hand."

her mane silky, long, and as full as possible.

It helps if your horse is well behaved, although being perfect isn't essential. But if your horse won't stand still for even one minute, the judge will not be able to see his conformation. Very nasty behavior such as bucking or rearing is unacceptable. If this happens and you cannot control it immediately, you must excuse yourself and leave the ring.

◯ What to Practice

Most important, learn where to stand while showing your horse to the judge. Never block the judge's view of your horse with your body; always move around to keep out of the way. Teach your horse to stand still, although you can make little adjustments as the judge inspects your horse. Practice this at home by having a helper walk around your horse as if she were the judge at the show. (Be sure your friend is careful not to walk behind your horse, though.)

Learn how best to show off your horse according to his breed. Morgans, Saddlebreds, and Arabians, for example, may be expected to "park out" in a stretched-out position. Stock breeds such as Quarter Horses and Appaloosas should stand square and straight.

Showmanship

Showmanship, like halter class, is done in hand. But instead of evaluating your horse, the judge looks for how well you show your horse. You will be asked to perform a preset pattern around cones or other obstacles. You may have to back your horse through two parallel rails or through a corner. You'll need to memorize the pattern before each showmanship class. It will be posted near the secretary's booth.

➲ How to Catch the Judge's Eye

Make sure your horse is well behaved and perfectly groomed. Know how to show him off at his best, how to highlight his strengths and underplay his weaknesses. Stay alert to the judge, and wear neat, well-tailored clothing.

➲ What to Practice

First, make sure your horse knows what is your space and what is his space. You won't be able to do showmanship patterns with your horse if he is walking all over you. Practice lots of

In a showmanship class, you must know how to emphasize your horse's good points.

turns with your horse turning away from you, not into you. And make sure he moves when you move at the gait you request. Avoid a lot of "clucking"; after watching many competitors all day, a judge can find this annoying. Use the energy in your body to increase the energy in your horse.

Pleasure

Pleasure classes evaluate your horse under saddle. They are intended to show your horse's three natural gaits — walk, trot, and canter (or walk, jog, and lope in Western classes) — and how enjoyable your horse is to ride at these three gaits. Your horse should pick up his gaits easily and look comfortable to ride at each of the gaits.

These classes are usually pretty simple (notice I said "simple," not "easy"!). You start at a walk, speed up to a trot/jog, then go into a canter/lope (or sometimes go back to the walk and pick up the canter/lope from there). Then you turn around and do the same thing heading in the opposite direction.

Once this "rail work" is done, everyone usually lines up in the center. One at a time, the riders are asked to back their horses. Then the judge marks the winners, and the class is over.

How to Catch the Judge's Eye
Since this class is all about the horse,

Your horse should look like a pleasure to ride in order to place well in a pleasure class, which is judged on the horse.

the judge wants to see a mount that is responsive, relaxed, and well trained. Conformation is not important, but your horse must have smooth, comfortable gaits and nice manners. When gait changes are requested, your horse must move into them quickly and willingly. He must be able to move freely within the group without getting cranky.

The judge wants to see a pleasant-looking horse and rider who appear to be enjoying themselves. Your horse can't smile, but you can! This is a simple way to give the illusion that you are enjoying the ride, even if your stomach is completely in knots.

What to Practice
Transitions between gaits are very important in a pleasure class, so do lots of them at home. Work on making your aids as invisible as possible and having your horse respond smoothly and quickly. If it's your or your horse's first time competing, try to create the conditions of a show ring when you train at home. Ask a few friends to help you practice by riding up behind you and passing you as you ride on the rail to help your horse get accustomed to having horses passing him. Judges may come up with things that you've never done, so be prepared to try anything.

Equitation

Like pleasure classes, equitation classes also show your horse at the walk, trot, and canter, but here the judge evaluates your ability to ride properly.

How to Catch the Judge's Eye

Equitation classes usually have a pattern you need to perform individually, usually in the ring by yourself. The judge will watch to see if you show the proper form for the seat you are riding, if you post smoothly and on the correct diagonal (rising when the horse's front outside leg goes forward), and if you canter comfortably on the correct lead. You should be in complete control of your horse at all times and able to maneuver in a group situation.

What to Practice

As with pleasure classes, your aids should be as unobtrusive as possible. You and your horse will benefit from lots of practice in the ring. Get help from a good rider if there is something you have difficulty mastering.

In equitation classes you are judged on your riding skills, including things like passing on the correct diagonal and maintaining good posture.

Trail

The classes discussed so far are the subjective ones (see page 18). Trail classes are one of the objective classes. You ride through a group of obstacles in a preset pattern and either you make it through each obstacle or you don't. Obstacles and challenges can include wooden bridges, water crossings, cavalletti, mailboxes that you open and close, a tarp that you step over, a rain slicker that you pick up and wave around, and so on.

Trail classes take a lot of time. For small to medium-sized shows, the trail classes usually take place in the afternoon and often in another ring while the rail classes continue to go on.

The trail course will be posted early in the morning so you have time to memorize the pattern. Learn the pattern cold — you should be able to ride it as easily as you find your way through the maze of corridors and stairs to your locker at school. The better you know the pattern, the more relaxed and confident you will be.

Patterns of rails may be among the obstacles presented in a trail class.

How to Catch the Judge's Eye

You and your horse should be confident and comfortable together, and your horse should be well behaved and willing. It's okay if your horse goes through an obstacle looking a little suspicious. As long as you negotiate the obstacle without knocking something down or stepping outside ground rails, you won't be marked off much, if at all.

What to Practice

Trail classes are fun to practice for, because nearly anything you do is good experience — not just for the show, but to improve your relationship with your horse. Set up your own obstacle course: a wading pool, a tarp, a sturdy wooden platform, a couple of logs. Accustom your horse to stepping on things, stepping over things, and stepping around things. Do everything slowly and expose your horse to each thing a little at a time. For instance, practice taking your jacket off while you are standing beside your horse and get that down pat before attempting it while you're in the saddle. Backing up is an important element of trail classes, so work on that. Actual trail riding is great preparation, too, and breaks up the monotony of ring work for you and your horse.

Profile: From the Judge's Point of View

How does a judge decide on a winner in a big class? AQHA (American Quarter Horse Association) Judge Carla Wennberg has competed for 30 years and is a 17-year veteran judge who trains other AQHA judges. She explains that "in the ring, the judge is making ten-second decisions. I group a class as it goes along into top, middle, and bottom." From there, she works her way to the winners.

Carla looks for many things, including:

◆ A nice expression on the horse, showing that he is willing and happy to be there, not cranky, sour, and forcing every step

◆ Good collection, with the horse balanced and flowing, and not being held together with the reins alone

◆ Consistency – you and your horse make transitions immediately and smoothly and remain a smooth, organized package throughout the class (more on this below)

Sometimes "pilot error" can eliminate a contestant. The rider simply does something wrong. You can't plan for that in your training program, but you can condition and practice until each element of a class is second nature to you and your horse. But sometimes you make a mistake. If the judge sees it, you fall to a lower grouping.

According to Carla, consistency wins more classes than action. Your horse may not be the prettiest mover in the group, but if you and he are a solid team, you will greatly improve your chances of earning a ribbon. Consistency means:

◆ Immediately changing gaits when asked – every time

◆ Keeping a steady rhythm in every gait, not speeding up on the long stretch

◆ Maintaining a positive expression on both you and your horse

Carla lists four things she looks at as she makes her decisions.

1. Way of going: Your horse should move smoothly.

2. Broke and quiet: no antics, refusals, or naughtiness!

3. Easy, smooth transitions: Your horse should move between gaits smoothly, not choppily.

4. Functionally correct: Your horse should be built to do the job at hand without conformation flaws that make it difficult for him to do what is being asked of him.

Jumping

Pleasure shows often have "working hunter" classes. In these English classes you ride in hunter attire and saddle. If you are interested in jumping, look for classes called "hunter over fences." The jumps are usually not very high and resemble the natural obstacles you might encounter while foxhunting, such as fences, logs, streams, and just plain jumps.

➔ How to Catch the Judge's Eye
The judge is evaluating how you and your horse look over fences and how willing your horse is.

Show Jumping

Show jumping classes take place in a ring as opposed to out on the cross-country course. The jumps are usually very attractive and are laid out in a pattern. Some jumps can be very creative as well as attractive — the huge shows like Devon have giant Shamu the whale statues or floral displays with enough plants to fill your backyard. As you move up in the jumping

To be successful jumping, your horse needs to be bold, very forward, and physically fit.

world, the jumps can get very high! This is where it can be helpful to have a tall horse, although some small and even pony-sized horses jump as if they have springs on their feet.

Many pleasure shows and smaller shows have a couple of jumping classes as part of the show. Other shows are completely dedicated to show jumping. There are also three-day or three-phase events that include show (or stadium) jumping as one of the three phases (along with dressage and cross-country).

➔ How to Catch the Judge's Eye
Jumping classes are strictly objective — you either jump "cleanly" or you make a mistake. Your horse may refuse the jump all together or he may just knock down a rail or two as he goes over the jump. You accumulate faults as you go around the course: four faults for each rail you knock down. You also receive faults when you exceed the time that has been marked as the maximum time for completing a course. A round with no faults is called a "clean" round.

➔ What to Practice
Obviously, going over jumps is important, but be careful not to overdo it or your horse could become stale or even injured. Mix up your jumping practice with ring work. It is especially good to work on transitions and making small circles — the approach to the jump is as important as the jump itself.

Show Story

Janelle has wanted to show horses as long as she can remember. Her mother shows and Janelle began right off in lead line before she even started school. For the past two years she has been getting into jumping. But she feels like no matter how many lessons she takes and how many shows she enters, she just isn't improving. There is some missing piece.

Her horse, Beastie, is willing and so is she, but many times they miss their take-off point and knock down the top rail. Or she overshoots the line to the jump and has to adjust last minute, losing time and setting herself up to be even more likely to knock down a rail. She and Beastie do great at home, but in the show ring with unfamiliar jumps, she can't seem to make it work as well, never placing higher than third.

One rare weekend she didn't have a show and went to a show with her friend Ray. Ray likes horses too but he's into Western stuff and likes learning about roping and working cows. While they watched the cow working classes, Ray explained what was going on. He talked about how the horse "rates" the cow, judging how far the horse has to stay behind and beside the cow to allow it to keep moving but not get back to the herd. And he talked about when it's appropriate to get out of the horse's way and let the horse do the job you're asking it to do. And suddenly something clicked. Maybe Janelle needed to do the same with Beastie and the jumps. Maybe she was just getting in Beastie's way.

Janelle couldn't wait to get home and try her new way of thinking. And it worked! Not every single time – they occasionally fell back into their old pattern – but whenever Janelle thought to herself, Get out of his way, Beastie was able to line up perfectly and sail over the jump!

You really can learn from something that seems completely different from what you are trying to do. Now Janelle watches dressage classes and even the pleasure classes with more attention. That afternoon at the cow working with Ray was a real breakthrough, and now she never passes a field of cows without yelling thank you!

Games

Barrel racing is a fast-paced class most commonly found either at gymkhana shows or at rodeos. Sometimes there are barrel classes at an all-around pleasure show. You must follow a pattern around several barrels within a specific time frame.

Western reining requires a smart horse and a sensitive rider.

➡ How to Catch the Judge's Eye

The cleanest run in the shortest time wins, so hang on!

➡ What to Practice

Although practicing going around barrels is important, just working on turning is very helpful. You tuck your horse into the barrel and pivot around it without knocking it over in order to avoid wasting precious time swinging wide around the barrel. Your horse needs to be very responsive to your aids, so teach him to respond when you ask for a turn or for more speed. And you both need to be comfortable going as fast as you can, so practice being both fast and smooth at the same time.

Divisions

Each show circuit has divisions in which you can compete. These can vary from circuit to circuit, but here are the three basic categories for young riders.

Youth

Youth divisions are age-specific. Often there are two categories in the Youth division: 13 and under and 13 to 17. A rider over 18 is usually classified as an adult and rides in the Adult division. The littlest kids, who can also have fun at horse shows, sometimes have "lead line" classes. An adult walks the horse on a lead rope, but the small child in the saddle still needs to sit properly and hold the reins and do everything else (wearing a helmet, of course). The adult is there just for safety.

Novice

Both youths and adults can be part of the Novice division. *Novice* means "new" and is a great way for you to get your feet wet along with a bunch

Your horse deserves a kind word at the end of the show day, no matter how many ribbons you did, or didn't, win.

of other riders, adult or youth, who are also new to showing. Don't worry, the adults in the Novice classes are just as nervous as you are! Sometimes there may be separate classes for Novice Youth and Novice Adults or the classes may be Novice Open, meaning it is open to both youth and adult novice riders.

Amateur

An Amateur division is usually a step up from the Novice division. You cannot be considered an amateur if you make money in any way from showing horses (the USEF does allow you to teach and still be an amateur). Training, being paid to ride other people's horses, and coaching others all put you in the professional divisions.

There's Plenty More

There are many more class possibilities besides the ones listed above. And many of these have different variations depending on the show circuit you become involved with. That's what keeps horse showing interesting and challenging.

Memorizing Tips

To memorize something like a class pattern, make a word association game out of it. If you can't make a word or phrase out of the initial letters of the obstacles or jumps, use some of your friends' names to help.

For instance, if the trail course pattern is to go through the cavalletti, go around the barrels, pick up the slicker, get the mail, then open the gate, you might think of some names of your good friends, like Carly (Caveletti), Bridget (Barrels), Susan (Slicker), Mary (Mail), and Gaylene (Gate). Don't forget, though, that you also need to remember the required gait between each of the obstacles, so you might end up with: Walk to Carly, Trot around Bridget, Stop at Susan, Walk to Mary, Canter to Gaylene, Trot to Exit Gate.

Another trick that really works is to trace the track on the paper with your finger. Tracing it twice is even better!

Whatever trick you pick, don't make it too complicated! It may be easy to remember something com-plex when you are standing in front of the secretary's booth looking at the map of the course. But that trick may be too confusing to remember when you are performing alone in the class and all eyes are watching you and your horse maneuver through the obstacles.

Allow plenty of time to read instructions and patterns before your class.

THREE

Who's Who:
Show People

A horse show is a complicated event to pull off. You will notice many official-looking people wandering around the show looking very busy — and they are busy! You will deal with some of these officials simply to sign up for the show. Others are working behind the scenes to keep things running smoothly. Still others are important to know about when certain situations arise.

Here is a sampling of some key people who organize and manage horse shows. Being a good competitor means following the rules, and these are the people who can help your show go well.

Be Organized!

"Send photocopies of Coggins and registration papers with your entry form, in advance, with a check, and they will love you in the booth."

– Cindi Adams,
show secretary

In the Secretary's Booth

Somewhere on the horse show grounds, usually close to a show ring, is a small building that the officials of the show call home base but which is known to everyone else as the secretary's booth. Any show personnel that you might need to contact will probably be in this booth; if not, someone here will know where that person is.

The Show Manager

The job of the show manager is to make sure that the show proceeds smoothly. Most of this person's real work comes before the show day itself. You probably won't be in contact with the show manager.

The Secretary

The secretary, who keeps track of entries for the show, is important to a competitor. If you need an entry form, contact the show or club secretary. If you have a question when you are filling out your entry form, the secretary will have the answer. You send the entry form back to the attention of the

secretary (keep a copy for yourself) if the show requires that you enter classes in advance. (Sometimes you receive a price discount if you enter ahead of time.) The secretary will be very busy the day of the show, so have your questions answered ahead of time if possible.

The Announcer

The announcer is the person you hear over the loudspeaker. He or she announces when competitors should begin heading to the gate for the next class, when the class is closed, and who the ribbon winners are. The announcer also gives important information like schedule changes, safety concerns, or cancellation of a class for lack of entries.

Competitors don't usually speak with the announcer directly, but the secretary or someone else in the booth can pass along information for him or her to read — for example, if a competitor needs a hold on a class for a tack change. Most important, the announcer passes along the judge's instructions, like gait changes, to the riders in the class.

Pay close attention whenever you hear an announcement, whether you are inside the ring or not. And keep

The judge makes decisions and tells the ring steward, who tells the announcer.

an eye on the ring itself, just in case the announcer doesn't announce that a class is starting soon.

The Ring Steward

The ring steward's primary job is to assist the judge and keep the class moving along, but he or she occasionally helps competitors as well. If you drop your riding crop on your way to the rail before the class begins, the ring steward may offer to pick it up for you so you don't have to dismount and mount again. The ring steward checks that everyone's number is showing, counts as riders enter the ring, and informs the announcer when to announce that the class is closed and the judging is beginning.

During the class, the ring steward closely follows the judge and takes instructions from the judge to pass along to the competitors. He or she also brings the judge's signed card to the show booth for announcement of the winners of the class. Pay attention to the ring steward when you are in a class.

The Judge

The judge, of course, is the person who chooses the winners of the classes. Small, one-day shows usually have just one judge. In a large show that combines several disciplines, there may be more than one judge — different ones for Western and English events, or perhaps one for jumping classes and a different one for flat work.

The judge usually does not give commands when riders are on the rail but communicates with the ring steward, who uses hand signals to relay the commands to the announcer. However, when you are lined up at the end of the class, the judge may ask you to back your horse. Most times, the judge simply gives the ring steward instructions about how he or she wants the class to be run, and the ring steward or announcer tells the competitors what to do next. This allows the judge to focus on the riders and their horses, watch transitions between gaits, and not miss any details.

Some judges, especially in smaller shows, youth shows, or classes with small numbers of entries, take time to tell competitors about the things they did especially well and the things a rider and her horse need to work on. Listen carefully when she is giving you this information — it will help you a lot in future rides! Be sure to thank the judge for taking the time to talk with you, even if he or she is critical.

Whom Do I Ask?

Some things come up only once in a while, so you may not know whom to ask about them. Here are some of these occasional but important questions and concerns that probably will come up at least once in your show career, so you will know how to deal with them.

Occasionally a judge will comment on your performance. This is valuable on-the-spot feedback, whether you are a novice or an advanced competitor.

Have helpers standing by to assist with your tack change.

If you have requested a hold on a class so that you can change tack, have the tack for your next class waiting not far from the exit gate of the ring so other competitors and show personnel won't have to wait long. Even better, have a pit crew waiting to help you make the switch. It's a good idea to practice the pit crew change so that you know exactly what each person's job is, and so that your horse learns to tolerate all those people busily moving around him.

Class Hold for Tack Changes

If you ride in more than one discipline on the same horse or even on different horses, there will someday be a time when you are entered in two classes in different disciplines, one right after the other. Since show personnel work hard to keep classes moving right along, the typical break between classes is only long enough for riders from one class to leave the ring and the riders for the next class to file in safely. You will need to ask for a "hold" on the next class to give you enough time to change your horse's saddle, bridle, and maybe even your own clothes. Go to the secretary's booth to request a hold on a class. Do this at least two classes in advance of the one you want the hold on. The class will not begin being judged until you and everyone else are in the ring and the class is considered closed.

Something Wrong with the Stall or Barn

Barns, stalls, and the grounds in general on which horse shows take place get used pretty hard. If your horse's stall door doesn't close or open smoothly, the water faucet is leaking, or a board in your horse's stall is broken, immediately go to the secretary's booth and inform the grounds manager.

For smaller problems, you can alert any show personnel, who will relay the information to the right person, though the repair may not get fixed until after the show. For these smaller problems, such as missing bucket hooks or hay racks, you will have brought temporary replacements,

Show Story

Throughout junior high school and high school, Louise spent most of her weekends at one horse show or another. She was often frustrated with all the paperwork. A lot of times her mother bailed her out when she forgot until the last minute to submit some form or another. Louise thought all the paperwork and rules and regulations were kind of silly and a bit of overkill.

In her mid-20s, after graduating from college, getting married, settling down in a house in her hometown, and starting a family, Louise got the horse bug again. But with small kids, she didn't feel ready to have a horse of her own. So she decided to volunteer to help with the local club, which put on several horse shows a year.

Wow! Now she realized how important all that paperwork is. Pulling off a horse show was no small project. It didn't even stop during the off-season – that's when all the meetings took place to plan the upcoming season.

Without all the proper paperwork and some specific rules that everyone needs to follow, the show, Louise quickly realized, would not be a success. She decided she would help kids understand this important behind-the-scenes aspect of showing. Each year well in advance of the show season, Louise puts on an information night to help kids sort through all the stuff they need to know but may not realize is so important to having a good show. They learn about making sure their horses have the proper vaccinations and the proper paperwork that shows they had the vaccinations; what Coggins tests are; how to make out the entry forms and when to send them in. And besides learning, of course they eat pizza!

such as bucket holders or hay nets — you're always prepared, right? (See the checklist in the appendix.) But the show personnel do want to know so they can repair these kinds of things.

An Unsafe Situation

An unsafe situation should be called to the attention of any show official as soon as you discover it. A hole in the ground that could hurt a horse or a person, protruding nails, a hanging door, a flood, or an electrical malfunction: These must be fixed immediately. If you don't know whom to ask or you can't find that person, ask any official and she will direct you to exactly the right person to tell or take that responsibility herself.

Disagreement with the Judge's Results

At least once and probably more often in your show career, you will disagree with the judge's results in pinning a class. Almost every time, you must keep that opinion to yourself — it is poor sportsmanship to complain about a judge's final results. If you just can't

keep it to yourself, discuss it with your very best show friend or your instructor or trainer or a parent. Under no circumstances, even for what you perceive to be a serious misjudgment, should you approach the judge.

If your parent or trainer feels it is something that needs to be taken further, let her discuss the situation with

show personnel. The rule book of the show's sponsoring organization will outline a specific way to approach the judge or lodge a complaint. If you don't have the rule book with you, check at the secretary's booth to find out the proper procedure to do this. Even a complaint warrants good sportsmanship.

Good sportsmanship means smiling when you don't win a ribbon as well as when you do.

Planning Your Show Season

Budgeting

You probably want to sign up for every horse show you see listed and every class that sounds like fun. But wait! How many shows will your budget realistically allow you to attend in a season? Can you go to a show every Sunday? Every Saturday and Sunday? How far are you able to travel in a weekend? And when you decide on the shows you can attend, how many classes are reasonable?

Have your mom or dad or riding coach help you fill in the costs associated with each show.

◆ Travel costs for you
(For example: hotel stays for overnight trips, meals, and gasoline or your share of the gas if you go with someone else)

_____

_____

_____

_____

◆ Travel costs for your horse
(For example: board for a stall on the show grounds, extra shavings, trailering by yourself or sharing with others)

_____

_____

_____

_____

_____

◆ Entry fees per class times the number of classes you would like to enter
(Use the discounted fee for mail-in entries on those shows you know in advance you will attend; use the non-discount fee on all others.)

_____

_____

◆ New tack or riding apparel you need for this year in any discipline

_____

_____

_____

_____

_____

_____

Scheduling

Ask yourself the following questions as you design your show schedule for the season:

◆ When will you and your horse be ready for your first show?

_____

_____

_____

◆ Do your parents have any family vacations planned during the show season? If so, when do you leave and return?

_____

_____

_____

◆ What is your total budget for showing your horse?

_____

_____

_____

◆ If you pay for your horse showing yourself, how many hours of show preparation and actual showing can you fit in each week around the time it takes to earn your showing money?

_____

_____

_____

Shows I Want to Compete In

Make a list of all the shows you want to attend this season. Now put them in order of priority. If you can't make it to all of them, you know which ones to concentrate your practice time and money on.

Show Name	Location	Date
1.		
2.		
3.		
4.		
5.		
6.		
7.		
8.		
9.		
10.		

PART 2

You and Your Horse

FOUR

The Right Horse

Choosing the right horse for you and for the discipline you prefer is an important part of successful showing. Take lessons at a horse facility that focuses on the kind of riding you want to do. If you like it enough, you can then look for a horse that will be a good partner for you in that discipline. You don't want to have spent money on and fallen in love with the perfect barrel racing horse only to find that barrel racing is no longer fun.

Take lessons at a riding academy that specializes in instruction for young riders. This approach has lots of advantages.

Size It Up

"Be sure you and your horse are a good fit. It won't guarantee you ribbons, but a horse and rider who are in good proportion are pleasing to a judge's eye. And when there are dozens of riders in a class, every little bit counts."

– Carla Wennberg, *AQHA judge*

Why Choose a Youth Riding School?

◆ A youth riding academy will have various horses that are suitable for your size and level of riding.

◆ Usually you can purchase a package of lessons, which is often less expensive than if you pay an hourly rate for individual lessons.

◆ You will probably ride with other kids your age and at your level.

◆ Many academies bring their riders to horse shows throughout the season. You can sign up to go to some or all of them.

◆ If the barn is big enough, they may host a few shows at their facility each year.

◆ You will have automatic access to people who know about showing and can help you at shows.

◆ You can probably show with the horse that you take lessons on and are comfortable with. This is the next best thing to owning a horse yourself!

Leasing

You don't have to own a horse; you can lease one. Academies and riding stables often offer partial leases on the horses they use for lessons. Usually, you pay some amount of monthly board in return for riding the horse three or four times per week. Sometimes the partial lease also includes one lesson a week. Someone else may be partial leasing the same horse, or he may be used for lessons during times you aren't scheduled to have access to him. This is one way that lesson barns can afford all the horses they need.

If you partial-lease a horse in a barn that doesn't show, ask before you lease if it is okay to take your leased horse to a horse show. If it is, you will have to plan ahead so that your horse will be available on the days that you plan to show. If you lease a horse from a barn that is a riding academy for kids, this probably will be part of the arrangement.

There are other ways of leasing horses. Often when high school riders graduate, they look for someone to lease their horse while they are away at college. Women equestrians who are having a baby may want someone to use their horse while they are pregnant and while they are busy the first few months after the baby is born. Sometimes this kind of leasing arrangement requires that you keep the horse at a certain barn. If you find a horse to lease but want to keep it somewhere else, don't be afraid to suggest that. As long as the barn you want to keep it at has a great reputation, you may be able to make the deal.

You will want to make sure you have a written contract that covers all the fine points of what is expected of you. What does the owner want you to feed the horse? Can you take it to shows? Who pays for routine veterinary care? (Probably you.) Who pays for emergencies and who makes decisions about medical care? And, heaven forbid, what happens if the horse dies while you are leasing him? Your parents should have a lawyer look over the contract to make sure everything is covered.

A Horse of Your Own

At some point, if you are serious about your equestrian pursuits, you will want a horse of your own that no one rides except you (and maybe your trainer). Buying a horse can be a lot of fun. But you must be careful in your selection. Owning a horse is a huge commitment, so it's important to find the right one. How do you know what to look for?

If you have already become involved in showing, you will have two advantages:

1. You have an idea of what kind of showing you would like to do.

2. You have a relationship with a trainer or coach who can help you find a suitable horse. Not only will she be able to come with you to look, but she will also know some horses that are for sale. There is a cost for this service, however. And you need to be sure your coach or trainer is thinking of your best interests, not her own — like trying to persuade you to buy a horse that you will need to pay her to train.

Keep in mind that as you look, you will probably not find the "perfect" horse. The only perfect horses are the ones you buy in a box with Breyer marked on the front! But if you figure out what your priorities are, you can find a horse that fits your needs. Then you can decide whether it matters that he has a parrot mouth or high withers or that he's not your favorite color.

What Are Your Priorities?

Whether buying, leasing, or simply riding, what is important when it comes to getting a horse for your chosen show discipline? That depends on the discipline. Are you showing in hunter/jumper shows? Then a priority is to select a horse that is willing, forward, and does not balk at jumps. If you plan to do Western pleasure shows, you don't need to spend your time looking at high-stepping "park" horses.

Once you've determined your priorities, look for a horse whose training exceeds your own riding level. Find a horse that is somewhat more educated than you are so you can learn from him without having to worry

about losing control or becoming frustrated because you don't know how to tell him what to do.

Another reason to choose a horse that is more experienced than you is that your level of competition will be a piece of cake for him, which allows you to relax and focus on your riding. He can help you become better at your current level. And his knowledge will make you ready and eager to go to the next level.

Don't fall in love with a horse until he has had a vet check.

Once your horse or pony takes you through the levels he knows, you will be ready to learn the next level together! Your coach can help you decide whether your horse has what it takes to move up.

Despite this advice, you don't want a horse that is used to competing at a much higher level than you are ready for. For one thing, a very high-level horse is likely to be out of your budget, but more important, you want a horse that will be your partner and trusted companion. A horse that can compete at a Grand Prix show but is being taken through beginning dressage tests week after week will probably become bored and restless and might not be much fun to ride.

Whatever discipline you choose, the right horse for you will have certain characteristics. His size should make you feel comfortable, both in the saddle and on the ground. He should respond easily to your signals and respect you. He should behave around other horses, be able to stand quietly in the ring or while tied, and load and unload calmly.

The Vet Check

You think you have found the right horse for you. The price is within your budget, and your coach thinks he is a good prospect for your skill level and your plans. Now what?

When you are serious about a specific horse, you will want to have a "vet check" done on him. Your veterinarian will work on your behalf and examine the horse to tell you his health status. She will also point out anything about his health or conformation that would make him unable to perform in the discipline you have chosen. A **farrier** (horseshoer) can also help with this exam.

Some people skip veterinarian exams because they cost a few hundred dollars. Account for this cost in your shopping budget for your horse — it's worth it! If you have a $4,500 budget, look at horses listed in the $4,000-and-under range and reserve the $500 for the vet check. You don't want to spend your whole budget on veterinary exams, so go this far only if you are really ready to buy this horse if the exam goes well.

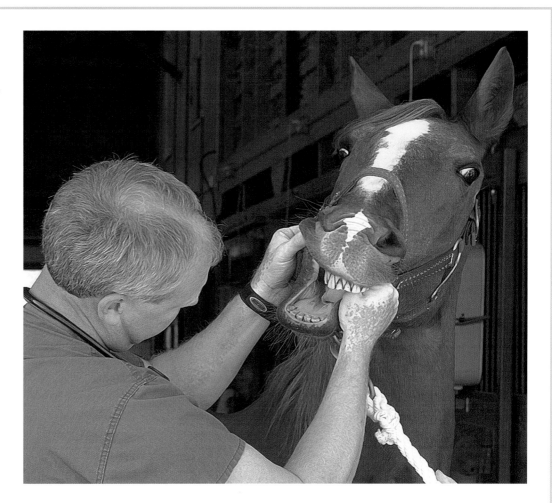

Don't fall in love with your prospect until after the vet check! The veterinarian may discover something that makes the horse unsuitable for you. It's hard to grow attached to a horse and then have to decide not to take him home. But you don't want to end up with a horse that isn't healthy, sound, and appropriate for you. Both you and the horse would be unhappy.

Show Story

Buying horses can be very emotional. Wanda learned that lesson the hard way. She fell in love with practically every horse she saw. And when she saw Brody, she knew he was the horse she had to have.

Unfortunately, the vet check didn't fare so well for Brody. He had been lame and the vet couldn't find the problem. It would have been better if he could. At least they would have known the cause of the lameness and been able to do something about it. Wanda hoped that the lameness was just temporary, and that if the vet couldn't find the cause, then it probably wasn't serious. Besides, Brody had good days when he wasn't off at all.

But a lame horse isn't a good horse to compete with, even just in local shows. You never know if show day will be a good day or an off day. Wanda began to have to sit out shows. She was never going to be able to progress to the state level this way. Whenever she did show, someone always came up to her to tell her that her horse looked a little off. Poor Brody. What was she going to do with him?

Brody made out okay. Because Wanda's family had a small barn, she did not have to pay to board a horse she couldn't show. Wanda's neighbor had a nice pasture that Brody was welcome to keep mowed for her if Wanda just put up some electric fencing. It was right next to the barn, so he could come in out of the flies whenever he wanted.

Wanda acquired another horse – and this time she listened to the vet's advice. Now Brody had a companion; and when Wanda and her new horse were off showing or training, Brody didn't seem to mind because it meant there was plenty of grass to eat.

Vet-Check Basics

Your veterinarian will let you know:

◆ **if the horse is generally healthy.** Is he an appropriate weight for his breed, size, and age, and suitable for what you want to do with him?

◆ **if his teeth are well cared for and in good health.** If they are really bad, the horse will be underweight. Teeth that have lacked care probably won't stop you from buying the horse. But you will have to spend the money on extra dental care.

◆ **if he shows any signs of lameness.** It is up to you whether or not to have the veterinarian determine the exact cause of the lameness. Sometimes this can be very difficult (and expensive) to pinpoint. If the lameness is from something obvious — such as a visible abscess or a rock stuck in his shoe — then you may still want to buy him. But if the lameness is not obvious, you should walk away.

Sometimes the prescription for a horse lame from apparent tendon problems is to let it rest for a year; but at the end of that year, the lameness can show up again after you begin using the horse. It just isn't worth taking the chance that he will never be sound.

For some disciplines, there are specific health considerations. For instance, if you plan to jump your new horse, you should check for navicular disease. The navicular bone is a bone in the foot that can break down, causing pain and lameness. Navicular disease cannot be cured, and treatment is expensive. Even with careful nursing, many navicular horses can only be ridden lightly — no jumping or long rides. The disease usually worsens as the horse ages, so it's best to avoid buying a horse suspected of having navicular. If you are really interested in a horse but there's a chance it has navicular problems, spend the money to have an X-ray to confirm one way or the other. And be prepared to walk away.

Horse-Hunting Tips

The best way to find anything is to tell everyone you know what you are looking for. The same goes for buying or leasing a horse. Tell every horse person you meet that you are shopping for a horse. There are a lot more horses for sale than for lease, so if you want to lease, this is even more important. You never know when someone will say, "I know this woman down the street from me who just got a new job in the city and is really busy. Her horse was at second-level dressage. When I saw her in the store the other day, she said she really loves her new job but hates it that her horse is now idle a lot of the time. Let me ask her if she will consider leasing the horse to you."

Your new horse may be just down the street. You won't know until you spread the word! However, never give out your phone number to strangers. Be sure the people you tell are people you know. If you have a trainer helping you look, give your trainer's business number; be prepared to pay the trainer a commission on his or her assistance in finding you a horse. And it is helpful if your trainer likes your chosen prospect!

Safety Concerns

Be sure to keep your own safety in mind as you shop for a horse. Always bring your own helmet to wear when you try out the horse. Tell the seller that you want to tack up the horse yourself. You have to be able to handle him on the ground before you get in the saddle!

Always watch the horse being ridden by someone else before you mount up. And make sure the horse is ridden doing what the owner claims he can do — if it is advertised that the horse can jump 3'6", make sure you get to see the horse jump a course that high (although you don't have to try those fences). If the owner won't ride him, find out why. Just because that person is nervous about riding the horse doesn't mean you will be, but you need to know the whole story. If what you see makes you nervous, don't feel that you must ride. Don't worry about what other people think and don't be talked into it if you really don't want to. Perhaps if someone led the horse around for the first few minutes you're mounted you'd feel better. That's fine. You need to feel okay about keeping yourself safe!

Shopping Safety

Even when trying out a horse, always wear a safety helmet, properly adjusted.

Ask Yourself

Here are some questions to ask when you are looking at a horse for sale. Make a copy of this page and bring it with you. It's hard to remember everything when you get home, so write down the answers right away.

◆ When did you acquire this horse?

_____

◆ Where did you buy him?

_____

◆ What kinds of training has he had?

_____

◆ What have his winnings been? (You probably can confirm this online, depending on what circuit or club he won with.)

_____

_____

◆ What does he like to do best? What does he balk at doing?

_____

_____

◆ What kind of food and how much does he eat each day?

_____

◆ Does he load into a trailer easily? Is he calm while riding in one? (If you are serious about the horse, ask for a trailer-loading demonstration.)

_____

◆ Has he had any health problems? Has he ever colicked or had surgery? Has he ever been lame? If so, what was the lameness caused by?

_____

◆ Is he good in his stall? Does he get along with other horses? Does he respect fences?

_____

◆ Is he easy to lead and brush and handle in general? (Definitely try this out yourself!)

_____

◆ What kind of tack has he been ridden with in the past?

FIVE

Conditioning and
Training

You wouldn't just walk out the front door one morning and run a marathon — or if you did, you wouldn't expect to last very long! Instead, you would spend several months conditioning, strengthening your leg muscles, increasing your lung capacity, and training your mind. The same is true of equestrian competition, only you have to train yourself *and* your horse in order to perform at your highest level.

Both physical conditioning and mental conditioning are important. You don't want your horse to become bored, cross, or fearful. Learn to become aware of your horse's frame of mind as well as his physical fitness. One can have a great effect on the other.

Ride, Ride, Ride!

The most important thing you can do to maintain your horse's physical fitness is to ride. A lot. If you live in a part of the country where you take a break over the winter, start off gradually as soon as the temperature and the footing are reasonable. Begin with short rides at the walk and build up to long rides with lots of trotting. Trail riding is a great way to build strength and stamina while taking a break from the routine of the ring.

If you have to wait until the weather is warm enough to ride, however, the show season is probably about to begin as well. If at all possible, keep your horse in a facility with an indoor arena so you can ride during the winter months. Or perhaps you can trailer him there a couple of times a week to keep him in some sort of condition. If you keep your horse in some condition over the winter, you will be ahead of the game in the spring. Winter is a good time to take lessons that move you and your horse to the next level of competition. Just like having a show to prepare for, having a lesson motivates you to ride in the winter when it's cold and you have to stay in the ring.

Safety First

Here are a few things you can do to lessen your chances for a fall off your horse:

◆ Ride an older horse. Usually, a horse or pony under five years old is considered not suitable for a green rider. This doesn't mean that older horses won't buck you off or rear or spook and bolt — they sure might! With horses, there's always an exception. Even though older horses usually have a calmer approach to things than the youngsters do, some older horses have been treated poorly and have learned to be defensive. Look for one with show ring and trailering experience.

◆ Expose your horse to all kinds of distractions. Don't sneak around with him, worried that he'll see

Accustom your horse to every possible distraction.

that dog over there, or avoid riding him when the wind is blowing. Set up situations where you can teach him about potentially scary situations in a controlled manner so that when he encounters something new in the real world, he'll be able to handle it.

Take proper precautions when exposing your horse to new things. In the comfort of his home environment, acquaint him with all kinds of different experiences — dogs, motorcycles, big tarps, a flag, a flapping grain sack. Ask an experienced horse person to help.

The more confidence you and your horse have in each other, the better your performance will be. Working together to overcome scary situations is a great way to learn to trust each other.

◆ Practice, practice, practice. If your horse is completely familiar with what you will ask of him at the show, he will be comfortable even when he finds himself in new surroundings.

◆ Expose him to showing gradually. Don't haul your horse off to his first-ever show and sign up for 14 classes. In the beginning, you might take him to a show with no intention of competing. Just walk him around and let him take in the interesting activity. Teach him to stand tied to the trailer without fussing. If he does well, sign him up the next time for a couple of classes, gradually building up to a full day of showing. What's the hurry? If you enjoy showing, you will probably be in it for a lifetime.

Working with a Coach or Trainer

Even the top riders in the world still work with a coach or trainer. To succeed and move on to higher levels of showing, whatever the discipline, you will probably want to work with a trainer, too. Your lesson barn may have (or can recommend) someone who works with riders on the show circuit. Many lesson barns that work with kids are set up so that an instructor takes a group

A coach can help advance your show career.

of kids to shows all season long.

A trainer will not only help you improve your riding skills for your chosen discipline, but will also know the current trends in clothing and the current rules about horse tack, such

Show Safety: Red Ribbons

Horses use all sorts of body signals to "talk" to each other. They may give a grouchy look to let another horse know not to get too close. Some horses, however, will kick another horse that comes too close to them in the ring.

Your horse should be well **socialized** – that is, he should know how to interact with other horses – if you plan to show him. If he does tend to kick, work with him so he doesn't feel so defensive. However, you won't change that behavior overnight, so while you are eliminating his kicking habit, the universal signal to other riders to beware is a red ribbon tied at the top of his tail. If you see another horse with a red ribbon, give that team a wide berth when you come behind or pass them.

as what kind of bits are legal to use. A trainer can teach you little things like how to salute a dressage judge properly, how to maintain a good position along the rail in the pleasure class, and where to stand as the judge looks at your halter horse.

A trainer who works personally with you can be expensive. For that reason, you might consider joining a club or lesson barn where you can find that kind of benefit within a group. Then when you reach higher levels, you may be ready to consider a trainer for yourself.

Longeing

Longeing is the term used to describe working a horse in circles around you. Usually the horse is controlled by way of a long lead rope called a **longe line.**

If for some reason you can't ride, longeing is a good way to exercise your horse and work on your communication with him. It can also be a way to warm up your horse if he is a little frisky, especially during the winter months! Learn to longe a horse

properly before you try it on your own. First, watch someone whose horsemanship you respect. Then get that person to teach you how to longe your horse.

Here are some steps to take when you are ready to longe your horse yourself.

◆ Find a longe line that you like. Some are nylon, some are cotton; some have rubber "doughnuts" on the end, some don't.

◆ Wear gloves. Of course, you want to teach your horse to longe respectfully, but if he bolts or if he acts up while he is learning, gloves protect your hands from rope burn.

◆ If your horse is truly "halter-broke" (see page 74 for more on that), he should learn to longe fairly easily. You may have to use a **longe whip** (a whip with a long handle and lash) to keep him a few yards out on the circle at first. Never touch your horse with the whip; if you need to encourage him to move out, make a noise in the air or on the ground with it.

- Your horse should travel around you with a nice bend throughout his body that mirrors the circle.

- Practice lots of up-and-down transitions (walk, trot, walk, canter, trot, canter, trot, walk, trot) for improved conditioning and focus.

- Don't bore your horse to death on the longe line. Work him in both directions. Build up slowly until you reach a maximum of 20-minute sessions.

- When you are finished, lead your horse with the longe line neatly coiled. Hold the coil in one hand (but never wrapped around your hand) and the end attached to your horse in the other. If you use a longe whip and carry it to and from the barn with you, be very careful to hold the lash against the handle. You don't want to frighten your horse accidentally with the whip while you are walking.

Longe your horse in a fenced area in case you need to drop the line to keep yourself safe.

Longe Line Safety

Never wrap a longe line (or any line that is attached to a horse) around your hand or wrist. Always hold the longe line, lead rope, or reins so that you can drop them if your horse bolts and you lose control.

It may seem obvious, but it's worth mentioning: Longe your horse only in an enclosed ring. That way, if you do drop the line (either accidentally or on purpose), he will not be running loose with a 30-foot line flying behind him. Don't let the line sag. As your horse comes in to you, gather the line in loops so that he won't tangle his feet in it. Better yet, teach him to stand while you approach him.

Show Story

Keeping a horse fit for the level of showing you plan to do is a big task. It is also an important part of your horse's training, Sally was learning. She worked really hard at Snip's conditioning and knew that it included his feeding program as well as his physical fitness. She was also learning that she couldn't forget about Snip's mental conditioning as well.

Most days Sally and Snip worked alone in the ring at her house. Once a week, her instructor came and gave her a lesson. Occasionally, when

Sally's mother had time, they took Snip to the instructor's barn, but it was pretty quiet there, too, with only a couple of horses and three other students.

With all their schooling work, Snip looked beautiful – nicely muscled with a coat that shone from good food and exercise. They worked on walk, trot, and canter and some trail class obstacles. Snip did great at home. But once at the show, it was as if he were a different horse. He became very excited and Sally felt that if they hadn't drilled so much on things like trail, he wouldn't even be able to hold it together enough to go over a couple of cavalletti.

At one show, a judge mentioned that it would help if Sally worked on Snip's mind as well as his body. That's when she began to learn a little bit

about mental conditioning. She got to work. She spent time sacking Snip out with everything she could find – rain slickers, grain bags, even tarps. With the help of her instructor, who had begun to attend clinics by the very same judge, Sally was able to see Snip settle down mentally. Finally, when they went to shows, Snip began to look to Sally for comfort in the confusion, rather than whinnying and racing around excited about all the other horses.

Snip never did seem to grow fond of the show environment. But now when he started getting all excited, Sally had some things she could do that seemed to have an amazing calming effect on him. This was a turning point for Sally: She could now feel that she and Snip were becoming a real team.

Avoiding Ring Sourness

If your horse does nothing but ride around and around a ring all the time, practicing and showing, he will get **sour.** Behavior problems will crop up: He may become hard to catch, or go slowly through the motions, or go really fast so he can be done and left alone. Pages 60 and 61 list some things you can do to avoid making your horse ring sour.

Round Pens

Some people do what is called "free longeing," which is when your horse is loose but working in circles around you. The training tool called a **round pen** (a circular ring about 50 to 70 feet in diameter, often set up with movable panels) has made this loose work more popular. This method, however, can be used inappropriately.

The main purpose of working a horse in a round pen should be to work on the horse's mind rather than his body. You can use the small space to keep his attention on you at all times, to teach him to be more responsive, and to develop your ability to communicate with each other. "Round pen work" should never consist of running a horse around in circles until he is too tired to do anything else but stop and face you. If someone teaches you to do this, find another instructor. Always be sure an experienced person is nearby or helping you when you work with a loose horse in a round pen.

Although the original intention of round pen work was to work on the horse's mental fitness, it certainly can build physical fitness. Asking your horse for up-and-down transitions is always good for conditioning. Use the smaller space to experiment on directing your horse without using voice commands — use the energy and position of your body and see what happens. What does it take for your horse to break from a trot to a walk? Do you have to slow down your own body? What if you step a little toward his shoulder? Do you practically have to stand in front of him and wave your arms (don't actually do this!)?

Use the round pen to learn to work subtly with your horse. Find out how small motions on your part will change your horse's behavior. Then work on refining your movements to elicit the particular behavior you want, such as slowing from a trot to a walk or coming to a complete halt.

If you use a round pen only for physically conditioning your horse, save your parents or yourself a lot of money and just buy a longe line, put your horse on it, and use it to make a circle out of the square corral or large riding ring you already have.

Now let's find out more about why your horse's mental fitness is so important.

Mental Fitness

Don't be the kind of horse person who concentrates only on the horse's physical fitness and appearance! A neatly braided mane, a shiny coat, nice shoulder muscles, and painted hooves are easy to see, so many people focus just on that. It's not that appearance isn't important. However, your horse's frame of mind is at least as important as his physical condition. In fact, the two are very connected: A horse that is in good physical shape but is nervous, cranky, or bored won't give a good performance. On the other hand, a horse can be calm, willing, and eager to please, but be too fat or stiff to give you a good ride. With experience, you will find that a horse's mental state becomes as obvious to you as his physical fitness.

There are two crucial aspects to keeping your horse mentally fit. First, establish mutual respect by being consistent. Your horse will be more content if he knows the rules. For instance, don't feed him treats out of your hand and then punish him when he bites you. Teach him the rules up front. Feed him treats in his bucket so he doesn't need to figure out when it's okay to put his mouth on you and when it's not. Wouldn't you be frustrated if it was okay for you to talk on the phone for an hour one night but the next night your parents punished you for talking on the phone that long? We all like to know the rules so we can live peacefully. Your horse does, too.

Second, provide your horse with freedom of movement. Horses are huge animals. If you compare his size to yours, a horse in a box stall is like you living in your closet. You'd have enough room to turn around but that's about it. Considering that horses in the wild roam for miles every day, grazing as they go, you can understand how important it is for a horse to be able to move around if he wants to.

Our horses no longer graze and roam all day. Most of them have to live in stalls. But we can work with their nature to keep them from becoming too frustrated with the kind of life we have imposed on them. Here are some tips for allowing your horse to live with more freedom:

◆ Turn out your horse as much as possible. Be flexible about turnout time and pasture companions. Barns with lots of horses have to accommodate many different schedules and

Don't let your horse get bored!

equine personalities. If you are afraid his coat will bleach out in the sun, you can blanket him with a light sheet to protect it. However, after you bathe him the afternoon before a show, go ahead and leave him in his stall. Put down fresh bedding and a big pile of hay. If he spends most of his time outside, he probably will be happy to snuggle up in his stall for a night.

◆ Turn out your horse with other horses. Horses are extremely social animals. If you are worried about bite marks and other blemishes from playing, turn him out with horses whom he either ignores or can stand up to. You never see bite marks on the boss horse! If he can't be in the same pasture with other horses, at least try for neighbors in paddocks on either side of him.

◆ Don't use confining equipment, even when training your horse at home. A saddle, bridle, and rider are already a lot of confinement for a horse. Don't add things like tie-downs or martingales — learn how to bring down your horse's head through better horsemanship, not with a piece of leather that artificially forces it down. If your horse's mental state is good, you won't need a tight noseband or harsh bit to keep his mouth quiet. A busy mouth, like a busy tail, is often the result of a frustrated or troubled mind. If you can help him relax and focus, his tail and mouth will take care of themselves.

◆ Don't drill your horse into boredom. Look for ways to practice a lot without either of you getting sick of it. Who says everything has to be done in the ring? There are lots of things you can work on out on the trails — even dressage moves! Mix it up for your horse. At least put down ground rails, cones, barrels, or whatever you can think of in the ring, and create some interest. Horses are curious animals and they like a change of pace and activity, just like you do.

Warming Up

A gradual warm-up is important for both horse and rider. Even if you are young and flexible, you can benefit from making stretching into a pre-ride habit. Stretch the hamstrings by holding your palms against a wall and bending one knee. And when you mount your horse, walk on a loose rein for a few minutes before gradually working up to a faster walk and trot. Don't start right off trotting for 20 minutes. Let your horse limber up — you don't want to make him lame and not be able to ride him in the show!

Also, always warm up at the show, for at least a half hour before your class. Both you and your horse will perform better because of it. Be as courteous in the warm-up pen as you are in the show ring. And if you see anyone doing something in the warm-up arena that you feel is unsafe, leave the pen and tell an adult what is happening. The adult can decide if something further needs to be done. Don't approach another competitor yourself with criticism about what she is doing.

- Don't do all your training in the ring! This is important. There is absolutely no reason you can't work on shoulders-in or haunches-in exercises out on the trail. Always ride with a friend for safety. This also gives your horse some experience being ridden around other horses.

- Don't put your whole pattern together and repeat it over and over when you practice. For instance, if you are preparing for a dressage test, pull apart the test in pieces and work on the individual pieces. Maybe put it all together once or twice, but don't do the whole pattern every time you ride.

- Find out what it takes for your horse to let down or relax. If you are practicing in the ring and your horse gets really tight, take a break. Maybe get off, even unsaddle him. Wait for your horse to give a big sigh and then you can start again. Look for signs that this horse isn't necessarily the right

one for the intensity of showing that you have planned for him. Don't burn out a horse just for your own showing purposes.

- Keep learning. Always strive to be the best rider and strive for the best horsemanship you can achieve. Learn how to ask things of your horse in a way that is fitting to the horse, not just fitting to you. Your horse will appreciate it and you will get the most effort from him.

Work One Level Beyond Your Show Level

This may sound like backward advice, but if you are training at home for 3' jumps, don't sign up for 3' jump classes at the show. Compete in the 2'6" jumps.

The same goes for dressage: If you are training at Beginner Novice at home, you may only be ready to compete at the Elementary level. Each element will be harder at the show than at home, so always compete a little "behind" what you are training for.

Horses help keep your sense of humor!

Is Your Horse in Tip-Top Condition?

Top condition will allow your horse to perform well, to have the stamina not only for the performance but also for the strains of traveling on the show circuit. Assessing your horse's condition is an ongoing process. Always contact your veterinarian if you suspect something isn't right or want advice on how to keep your horse in good show condition. Here are a few tips to keep in mind.

1. On a non-show day, check your horse's temperature (normal 99-101 degrees), respiration (8-20 breaths per minute), and heart rate (normal 32-40 bpm) to get "baselines" on these vital signs so you will know if something is not in his normal range.

2. Always observe your horse's weight. If you can easily see his ribs, he is too thin. Too fat is as bad as too thin, but most heavily worked horses do not get overweight.

3. How does your horse's coat look? A shiny, even coat is the sign of a healthy horse; a patchy, dull coat means he needs some nutritional changes or grooming attention.

4. Check your horse's manure every day. It should form moist balls and not be too loose or too dry.

5. Always make sure your tack fits your horse. If it suddenly stops fitting, it may mean your horse is losing or gaining weight. A saddle that doesn't fit will make your horse sore and unable to perform at his best.

6. Sudden behavior changes can indicate a horse out of condition or not well. If he starts being grouchy when saddled when he always stood quietly to be saddled before, you should check his saddle fit. Sometimes, as horses gain condition in the show season, the saddle's fit changes.

7. Learn how to check your horse's recovery rate (the time it takes for all his vital signs to come back to normal levels) after a good workout. If you know people who do endurance riding, they will be able to help. Their conditioning technique of long, slow, and distance work can condition any horse.

8. If your horse is not ridden during the winter, always take it slow when conditioning him for the spring season. Gradually build up to the level of exercise that your horse will perform at during showing.

SIX

On the Road

Transporting your horse to a horse show almost always involves a horse trailer. If you show on your own, you will need to have one available to you, even if you don't own it. Businesses that rent large equipment sometimes have horse trailers, but you will have to book it ahead of time for all your shows so you don't get stuck when someone else rents it the same day you want it.

Perhaps another showing family might share the trailer rental with you, to help keep the costs down. Make sure the rental company is a reliable business that will maintain the trailer so it is safe.

Training and Traveling

"When you travel with your horse, the number one priority is for both of you to arrive safely. And when you train, encourage your horse to take one step at a time. Be patient and take the time to make your horse a deliberate, safe loader and unloader."

— Cherry Hill,
*trainer, author,
and longtime judge*

Buying Your Own

If you own a horse and show often, you should consider buying a trailer. Have someone who is knowledgeable about vehicles help you and your parents purchase one. Don't think you have to buy a fancy new rig! A modest used one can work just perfectly and be a great way to stay within your showing budget.

Whenever you trailer with someone else, notice what you like and don't like about the trailer. Maybe it doesn't have full dividers to keep two horses side by side from bumping into each other. Maybe the "escape" door is hard for you to open and close. These are things to write down and think about when it comes time for you to have your own trailer.

Trailering with Someone Else

If you board your horse at a barn that does a lot of showing, you and your horse will probably ride with other show people. Maybe the barn has a trailer that holds several horses and yours is one of four or six "passengers." If that is your situation, plan accordingly. Unlike having your own trailer, where you can keep your stuff in it and be ready to go all the time, riding with someone else means keeping your supplies portable. But it also means you don't have to own a trailer and be responsible for the upkeep.

Be prepared to pay for your share of riding in the trailer. Your costs will include gas and tolls and will depend on how many horses and riders there are. Always plan to do your fair share of the work keeping the trailer clean and well stocked for the show.

Trailer-Training Your Horse

If the horse you show is a seasoned show horse, he will probably walk into the trailer easily and ride calmly. When you have a new horse, however, you may need to help him become a seasoned traveler. Sometimes horses get a little sour about trailers.

Imagine your dream trailer, a true palace on wheels.

Your trailer is your home away from home at a horse show.

Before you buy, ask lots of questions of friends who have trailers. What do they like about their trailer? What do they wish their trailer had that it doesn't? For instance, maybe they bought a new trailer with a tack area but now wish the tack area had a saddle rack and a light. Sometimes little things can mean a lot!

Loading the Reluctant Horse

There's not much that is more frustrating than a horse that won't go into a trailer. And he usually is most stubborn about it when you are in a hurry. It's smart to perfect this part of your horse's show education when the pressure is off and you don't need to go anywhere.

Some horses simply need a buddy in the trailer for the first few rides to reassure them. If there is a horse going along who is a good traveler, load him first. You may find that your horse will then climb right in. Although he still has to learn to load by himself, sometimes loading a few times with a companion on board makes a horse confident enough to do it on his own. If your horse enters but won't settle down until another horse is on board, don't load your horse until the other horse is almost ready to join him or load him second. Again, even though you want your horse to become a willing loader and quiet rider, it is best not to let loading become a test of wills. Use whatever works to load your horse quietly.

These are short-term solutions to the reluctant loader. Always strive toward helping your horse load easily and ride calmly. It may be a matter of "road" experience. You can work at this between shows so that each loading session gets easier.

Trailer-Loading Tips

There are ways to improve your horse's attitude about loading. Always be sure to have an adult nearby to help if things get out of hand. A scared horse is a powerful thing!

Do not lead your pony by the clip right under his chin. If you led my Quarter Horse mare that way, she would try to bite you to tell you to back off a little! Horses, and even ponies, are big and need a lot of room. Teach your pony to be respectful of your space, then trust him and give him a little breathing room.

Hold the lead rope about a foot from the clip. Then, if your pony spooks at something while you are leading him, he has some room to move without yanking your arm out or jumping on top of you! Work toward becoming so aware of your pony that even when he is a foot or two behind you, you still know what he's up to. If you are afraid he is going to use the extra lead rope to dive for grass, teach him not to! Make sure you have a firm enough grip on the lead rope that if he did try to lower his head for grass, he would run into the end of the lead rope and not rip it through your hands.

Trailer Loading Step by Step

1. Let your horse check out the trailer for a few minutes before you ask him to climb in.

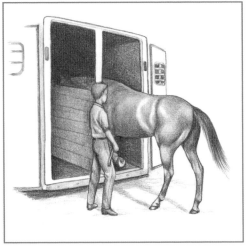

2. It's best to load a horse halfway and back him out a few times before getting him all the way in there.

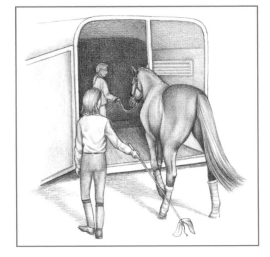

3. If after a while your horse doesn't respond to your request to go in, have a knowledgeable adult give him pressure from behind.

Before you begin trailer training, read "Homework Time" at the end of this chapter. What does all that halter work have to do with trailer loading? A lot! You can put the trailer in front of a horse, but if you can't direct the movement of his feet, you will not get a reluctant horse to load. If you can manipulate your horse with subtle signals, trailer loading will not only be easier but it will also be both fun and fascinating instead of frustrating!

Here are some other ways to practice halter work at home.

◆ You walk up to the trailer with your horse. You step up into the trailer and ask him to follow you in. He has other ideas and steps off to the side. What do you do? Step out, walk the horse away from the trailer, and turn around to line him back up again? No way! You will teach him that if he refuses to go in the trailer, he actually gets to walk away from it — definitely *not* what you want him to learn! If you can direct your horse's feet, you can make him line back up with the trailer without you moving at all.

◆ Let the horse find out that the trailer is a good place to be. Whenever he turns his attention away from the trailer, get him busy. Don't punish him, just get him working! Step his hindquarters over to either side of the trailer, move his front quarters across, back up, lead him around in a circle. After a few minutes, offer the trailer again.

The minute he is directed toward the trailer, become very still. This may take several tries, depending on your skill and your horse's individual personality, but eventually he will get the idea that away from the trailer is hard work and near the trailer is peace and quiet. And he will want to be in that quiet place.

4. If your horse just doesn't load into the trailer, go back to the drawing board with halter work, learning to direct his movement effectively.

5. Go off to the side to practice halter work. Your horse may soon associate the trailer with peace and quiet and climb right in!

- Once he understands that the trailer is a good place to be, ask for more. At first, he may just look into the trailer. That's fine. If he turns his attention away, give him a brief chance to come back. If he doesn't, or starts to back up, get busy again. If he looks in the trailer for a couple of minutes, that's great. Let him sniff the floor, smell the wall, hear himself snort in it. Then ask for more until ultimately he is in the trailer.

- Try "loading" your horse without the trailer. "Load" him through a stall door or alongside the trailer. Mimic the trailer experience as closely as possible.

- If you have trouble loading your horse in a two-horse trailer with straight "stalls," try a different kind of trailer. Borrow a stock trailer. While the experience of loading into a big open box doesn't exactly match that of walking into a more narrow stall, just getting into a trailer that he feels more comfortable with is a big step in the right direction!

- Sometimes one little thing can make a big difference. Does your horse seem like he would *like* to go in but is still hesitant? Does he stick his neck in as far as he can and sniff around but refuse to put his legs in? Try opening the "escape" door in the front. Sometimes that can make a dark trailer less scary. Always be careful, though, that he can't walk straight through and try to exit from a door made for humans, not horses!

- Use food as a reward but not as a bribe. Once a reluctant horse climbs into the trailer, have a treat of carrots or a handful of grain or hay there for him to relax with. But don't try to bribe your horse on with food. If he isn't hungry, food won't do a thing. Besides, your goal is for him to load into the trailer because you asked him to, not because you bribed him. This isn't too much to ask of your horse.

Traveling Tips

If you ride to the show with one or more friends and all of your horses in one trailer, have each person be responsible for at least one task that helps the whole group. Hang an erasable board inside the trailer's tack room door. Make a list of things that need to be done each time you travel. Assign a person to each task before every show. Rotate chores so that no one is stuck doing the same thing every time.

Hazards to Avoid

Loading a reluctant horse into a trailer can be dangerous. Both you and your horse can be hurt if he panics or fights you. Be calm, have a plan, and avoid the following things.

- Don't practice loading your horse in the trailer when you are alone. Always have someone close by to help if something goes wrong. Until your horse is reliable about loading, have an experienced horse person assist you.

Horses can learn to be calm and comfortable in a safe trailer that has sufficient room.

◆ Never hold hands with another person behind your horse or use a rope or board to "shove" him in. In the first place, no horse can be pushed into a trailer — people just aren't strong enough to do that. The horse will load calmly only if he understands your requests and feels support from you, not because someone is behind him. Don't put yourself in this dangerous position.

◆ Never tie or shut a horse in a trailer until he loads and stands calmly. The idea is not to ambush him or create a frightening experience, which is why you should practice loading before you need to go anywhere.

◆ Don't tie or untie your pony in a trailer until he has been blocked from behind with the "butt bar" or door. He should realize that he can't back up. If he feels open space behind him, he may try to rush back, which could be disastrous if his head is tied.

◆ Don't accept help from anyone unless you know him and trust his ability with horses. Loading a horse in a trailer can be a frustrating experience. You don't want someone helping you who has a short temper — someone like that will only upset your horse.

◆ Sometimes no matter how hard we try to stay calm, horses will make us angry. If you feel like you are getting angry with your horse as you try to load him, quit for a while and come back later or the next day. Make sure to quit on a good note, when your horse is at least standing calmly and looking in the trailer. Wait until you ask him to walk away, instead of letting him decide when to move. That will help you start calmly when you come back to the trailer later.

Although this girl is holding her horse a little close, he seems quiet and willing.

Note: Never help another person who is having trouble loading his horse unless he asks for your assistance. If you do help, remember that the owner of the horse is in charge. If you think anything that is going on is not safe for you or for the horse, express your concern and excuse yourself from assisting.

Wraps and Blankets

Does your horse need his legs wrapped and a blanket on when he's in the trailer? Well, like many things with horses, that depends. Even the slightest sudden move of the trailer can throw a horse off balance and injure him. If your horse doesn't have much experience riding in a trailer, wrap his legs until he learns how to balance himself. Many owners wrap their horse's legs whenever they travel, just to be on the safe side. If he has never had leg wraps on before, make sure he is comfortable wearing them before he rides in a trailer. If the leg wraps make him paw or bounce around, you may be causing more trouble than you avoid!

As for blankets, horses rarely need them in a trailer that is closed up tight. More than one horse in a trailer can make it very warm on board, even with windows open. In fact, always have some ventilation in the trailer, even when you think it's too cold. In the winter, a light blanket might be necessary if your horse is riding alone in a stock-type trailer — which has open slats near the roof — or if he is going to be standing in a parked trailer for any length of time.

Show Story

Mitsy, Jennifer's first horse, always walked right into the horse trailer. When Jennifer bought her new horse, Redwood, she was surprised to find that he was not as good about the trailer as Mitsy was. In fact, he was pretty bad. Jennifer wasn't sure what his previous owners did to get him in the trailer and to her barn in the first place, but whatever it was sure wasn't working for her.

A few times, Jennifer found herself almost in tears trying to load Redwood. People would help but they would do what Jennifer thought were dangerous things; she would get scared of getting hurt and Redwood would just get more upset. Jennifer read about an upcoming clinic not far from home that had a class on ground work that included loading a horse into a trailer.

As it turned out, the clinician had Redwood loading on and off in minutes. Then he handed the horse to Jennifer and said, "That's all well and good that I can load him, but you need to be able to do it too." He then showed her a lot of groundwork stuff that she could work on that would help. And while she tried to load Redwood doing what he had done, the clinician helped her with her position and timing.

Redwood's loading problem wasn't cured overnight or even in the three days of that one clinic. But the clinic helped Jennifer to come away with some understanding of Redwood's way of thinking and how she could help

him. Now, although it isn't as immediate as she would like it to be, Jennifer can load him into the trailer within a few minutes and neither one of them grows frustrated. The clinic was worth every penny!

Homework Time: Halter Work

The key to loading any horse is to have the horse thoroughly "halter-broke." In my opinion, just because a horse wears a halter does not make him halter-broke! Here are some questions for you.

◆ Does your horse respect your space?

_____

◆ Does he stop when you stop?

_____

◆ Will he move any foot in any direction at your request?

_____

◆ Does he stand still whenever there is slack in the lead rope? (If the lead is hanging on the ground, this is referred to as "ground tying.")

_____

◆ Does he move when you start to take the slack out of the lead?

_____

Check Your Horse's Halter Work

1. Stand on his left and begin to walk forward. Does he start to move before the lead rope gets tight? He should. A halter-broken horse will avoid the slack coming out of the lead rope. It means he has to pay attention to you every minute! This is not a bad thing to expect of a 1,000-pound animal who is attached to you by a rope.

2. Stand facing him on his left, put your hand on the lead rope near his chin where it meets his halter, and ask him to step backward. How hard did you have to ask before he started to back?

_____

Tip: A horse can feel a fly land on his rear end, so surely he can feel the slightest pressure on his head. Your job is to show him what you want. The second he starts to shift his weight back, relax the pressure on the lead rope. Start again and keep building in stages until he moves back swiftly with just a little pressure from you.

74

3. Stand on his left and bend his head in to you just a little. Does he bend readily, smoothly, and easily without you having to pull with all your might? If not, hold until he does, and the second you feel him bend at all, release the pressure.

Tip: Start again and if the timing of your release is good, each time you ask he will respond sooner.

4. Still standing on his left, bend his head a little more. Does he step his left hind foot away from you? If not, encourage him to do that by tapping on his left flank with your hand (stay in a safe position and don't get kicked!) or with the end of your lead rope or a crop (lightly!).

Tip: Do not stop tapping until he moves his hind foot. Then when he moves, stop tapping immediately! How many taps did it take? At first, be satisfied if he moves his foot slightly. Eventually, you want him to move his hind foot deeply underneath him when you bend his head more than a little.

5. Once he's moving his left hind foot at your request, you may want to add another element, which is to ask him to swing his front feet over to his left. To do this, you will need to get his head on the other side of you. Pick up your lead rope in your left hand, bend his head, and get a deep step with his left hind in front of his right hind. Ask him to rock his weight onto his back legs by slight backward pressure on the halter (just as you did when you backed him up).

Tip: Grab the lead rope with your right hand closer to the horse's head than your left hand, and direct his head to move to your right (at first you may need to put up your left hand to block him and help him move away from you and your hand and in the direction you are pulling his lead rope). He will rock his weight back and move his front feet to your right and be facing the opposite direction.

Once you have perfected this, you will find that you now can move your horse's four quarters in any direction and be fully in control of his feet at any time. This can calm down an impatient, upset, or frustrated horse. He can use up that energy moving his feet without having to go very far. If you come to understand this little exercise well, you will also understand how to do it from the saddle.

Be patient with yourself; it's a lot of coordination! And be patient with your horse; until you get smooth, he can get frustrated. Make sure he is far enough away from you that he doesn't accidentally step on you. Start teaching/ learning this in a calm environment where he isn't going to spook and accidentally run you over.

SEVEN

All About
Grooming

Grooming is a big part of caring for a horse. Not only does it make him look nice, but it also helps him stay healthy. Regular brushing rids the coat of dirt and bugs and other things that irritate his skin. It gives you a chance to check him from top to bottom for cuts, lumps, bumps, or anything unusual. And it is just plain quality time for you and your horse during which you can develop your relationship.

Daily grooming is important, but grooming for a show is at an entirely different level. Does it really make a difference to the judge? You bet it does! If two teams perform equally well, appearance can determine which one earns the blue.

Polishing and Pampering

"I loved grooming my horse before a show. I thought it was very important and so did my trainer. Although I don't show anymore, I still use all the grooming techniques I learned during my show years."

— Stephanie Levy,
Western Pleasure competitor on her Quarter Horse, Cody

Grooming Basics

Pay regular attention to the regular day-to-day grooming basics. That way, his coat and hooves are healthy and when a show is coming up you can concentrate on special treatments. Below are the basic tools and how you should use them.

Always wash your show brushes as soon as you get home so the tote will be ready for the next time. Wash your barn brushes regularly, too. To wash your brushes, first remove loose dirt and hairs (a metal currycomb is good for this). Then soak them in a mild dishwashing detergent. Scrub one brush against the other if they are really dirty. Rinse them completely and let them dry in the sun.

Types of Brushes

1. Use a rubber or plastic currycomb to go around in circles and raise all the loose hair and dirt on the body.

2. Use a stiff brush (not too stiff, though!) to brush out all the loose stuff that got curried up.

3. Use a soft brush to give your horse's coat a nice shine and clean his legs and face.

4. Use a mane and tail brush to remove shavings and bits of hay (don't forget the foretop!).

5. Use a hoof pick in the U-shaped groove around the sensitive frog at the center of the hoof.

Brushing Tips

Keep a tote or bucket stocked with your favorite brushes. In fact, you need two sets: one for the barn and one to bring to the show.

Level-Two Grooming

The next level of grooming goes beyond the basics: for example, if it's spring and your horse is shedding his winter coat; or if he has a knotted mane or tail after a day in the paddock with some playmates. Here are some "level-two" grooming ideas.

Shedding the Winter Coat

You will develop preferences for tools to brush out your horse's winter coat. Some of these shedding tools can be harsh, so your horse may have preferences, too! The simplest one is a rubber mitten with little nubs on it that collect the hair as you rub your horse down. It's great for dried mud, too.

The traditional tool is a shedding blade with leather handles on each end that clamp together to form a

"Spring cleaning" will give your horse the blissful feeling of a good massage.

circle. One side of the blade has teeth; that's the side to use for a winter coat. Use this side on your horse's body only, not his face, legs, mane, or tail. The other side is smooth; that's the side you use for baths.

Another kind of shedding tool is a rubber currycomb with longer, thicker prongs than a regular one. This tool can feel really good to your horse, like a massage. The hair col-lects in the deep areas between the nubs, so clean the "horsehair waf-fles" out as you go along.

A Tangled Mane

Long horsehair tangles fast. Even a windy day can do it. If pieces of hay get caught in the mane or tail, the hair tangles around that. It can be frustrating trying to brush out the knots and tangles.

Don't use a comb and pull on the knots, as you will be pulling out lovely hair that will take months to grow back! Use a spray or gel or lotion that is made for smoothing tan-gles out of manes and tails. There are several different kinds; try them until you find one you like, then stock up.

If your horse's mane is tangled, apply detangler on the mane before you start grooming. By the time you finish with the rest of his body, the detangler should have worked into his mane enough to make combing out the tangles easy. Now you can use a comb to smooth out the tangles — the combs that have teeth that rotate are great for this. Start at the bottom of the tangled area and ease out the snarl, working up as you go.

You might want to use rubber gloves (like the kind for doing dishes) when you work on a tangled mane because the detangler will make your hands very slippery. These products should work on even the toughest of tangles; it just may take a little more goo, a little more time, more hard work, or all three.

Staying Clean for a Show

The best way to keep your horse clean for the show is to bathe him the afternoon before the show, then put him in a freshly bedded stall until you load him into the trailer. But if the only time you can bathe him is a few days before the show, you may want to turn him out with a lightweight sheet to keep him clean. He probably will still roll, but the sheet will protect him from most of the dirt.

Manes and tails can be braided or banded to keep them as free of dirt and hay or shavings as possible. Using silicone sprays can keep the bits of hay from clinging. You can even use some of these products on your horse's body; just don't use them where the saddle will go — you'll feel like you're riding on a banana peel!

Face and feet can be easily touched up at the show before your first class. White hair (like socks and blazes) can be whitened with a little powder (watch the eyes!).

Burrs can be hard to remove. Try softening them with water and gently working them out with your fingers. However, if your horse has burrs in his mane and tail, the best thing would be to rid the pasture of burrs or block off the area where the burrs are. Burrs can also get in the forelock and then into a horse's eye, irritating the eye and causing it to swell.

The Tail End

Showing trends change, but a full tail is almost always in style. Take good care of your horse's tail. Brush it; don't comb it. Use conditioners to keep it soft, shiny, and tangle-free. Use bug spray when needed and worm on a regular schedule to keep your horse from scratching his tail on a post. This breaks the hairs at the top of his tail, which leaves him with a skimpy tail and a fluff ball at the top!

If your horse doesn't have a naturally full tail — or if his yearling pasture mate chewed it off — you can enhance it with kind of a wig, called a "fall." Falls are made of real horsehair, and you can buy one to match your horse's tail. They can be expensive, though, so use it only for the show. And if your horse naturally has a nice tail, it's worth taking good care of it.

Grooming at the showgrounds is a chance for you to relax and focus on your horse.

Grooming for a Show

You groom your horse regularly — at least three or four times a week, right? If you do, the extra grooming required for a show will be less work and more fun, and will make your horse look spectacular!

Once you really get good at grooming, you will come to enjoy figuring out how well you can spruce him up.

Mud

Horses love to roll in the mud — especially if you have just bathed them for a show! If the mud has dried, you can just curry it right out, but if it's still wet, you need a different approach.

Don't brush wet mud into your horse's coat — you'll just smear it around into his skin and dirty your brush. If you can, groom the rest of his body while the mud dries. If the sun is out or it's warm enough, it will dry pretty fast. Then you can just curry it out. Otherwise, wipe it off with a wet towel. Don't use too much water if the temperature is cool; use warm water to wipe off the mud and then dry him with a towel.

Rinsing well is the single most important step in bathing a horse.

Bathing

Your horse or pony must become very familiar with hoses and baths if you are going to have a show career together. For handling tips, turn to the "Homework Time" section in chapter 6. You need to be able to direct your horse's feet in order to accustom him to the hose. It can be pretty confusing trying to handle a moving horse and the hose without tangling them up, so if your horse is not "bath-broke," have someone experienced help you the first few times.

It helps to bathe your horse for the first time on a really hot day. Most horses will tolerate a bath with warm water, and many even enjoy it.

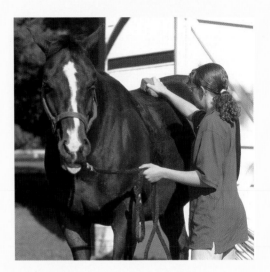

Bathing Your Horse

1. Curry out loose dirt and dried mud before you begin.

2. Don't use detanglers on the mane and tail until after the bath. You will just be rinsing them off!

3. Wet your horse thoroughly.

4. Apply shampoo to one side of your horse at a time. Use enough to work up a lather, but not so much that it takes hours to rinse out. If you show a lot, use very mild shampoos. Use shampoos marked MEDICATED only when your horse has a skin problem to be treated. Work up a good lather using your fingertips or a rubber currycomb.

5. THIS IS THE IMPORTANT PART: Rinse that side off. Really well. And when you think you've rinsed it enough, rinse it some more. You don't want to leave any shampoo suds in your horse's coat to dry and irritate his skin.

6. Repeat on the other side.

7. Rinse the whole horse again, since some of the shampoo from one side may end up over on the side that had already been rinsed.

8. Use a shedding blade, sweat scraper, or squeegee like the gas station attendant uses to wash your car windshield, and scrape off the excess water. If it's chilly out, towel down your horse or let him dry in the sun if it's out (keep him on a lead and graze him near some yummy-looking grass so he won't be so tempted to roll). If you are worried about bleaching your horse's coat in the sun, put a light blanket on him — his body heat will dry him off quickly.

9. Now it's time to tackle special areas like the ears, face, sheath or udder, and dock (be careful with those sensitive areas that are in kicking range!). Fill a bucket with warm water and use a facecloth or small towel to wipe these places clean. Don't use shampoo on your horse's face. You don't want to risk splashing lather or soapy rinse water in his eyes or ears. NEVER get water in a horse's ears.

10. Let your horse dry completely before you put him back in the stall or paddock. If he's still wet, the first thing he will want to do is roll! If your show is the next day, put him in his freshly bedded stall. You don't want to have a dirty, dusty horse ten minutes after the bath.

Clipping

Clipping a horse around the ears, muzzle, and fetlocks takes away some of the fascinating little protections that Mother Nature has provided to the horse. The hair in the ears keeps out flies, dirt, and water. The hair on the fetlocks directs the rain that runs down the horse's legs and protects his legs from scrapes. The muzzle whiskers allow a horse to feel the edges of things that are close to his head, an area where he cannot see well because of the position of his eyes.

For these reasons, clip the least amount that is appropriate for your discipline. Horses that don't show don't need any trimming. However, for showing, your horse must look neat and tidy, so you will have to clip some areas. How much you clip is up to you.

If your horse has never been exposed to clippers, take plenty of time the first time. Not only must you teach your horse to be comfortable with the clippers whirring around his ears, but you should also teach him to lower his head to a level that is comfortable for you to reach and see.

You may stand on a sturdy stool, but you will still need him to lower his head. Unless you use a huge ladder, your horse will always be able to put his head higher than you can see! If he's already an old pro, let's get started.

Use small-sized clippers made especially for clipping tricky places like the ears. Try not to let hair drop into your horse's ears as you move the clippers. If you prefer minimal

Cordless clippers can make it easier to trim ears.

clipping, just neaten up the hair that falls out of the edge of the ears and don't shave all of the ear hair. However, if your area of interest is showmanship or halter, you will need to be extra particular about clipping and aware of the latest requirements. For instance, over the years it has become more acceptable to let whiskers be an inch or so, not completely shaved.

Use the same small clippers to trim the whiskers off your horse's muzzle. Be very careful! The skin around the muzzle is tender, and there are lots of folds and creases that your blade can nick. Some people clip the whiskers leaving an inch or so, then tidy up the job with a disposable safety razor or a small pair of scissors. Be careful not to cut your horse or yourself!

You may be able to use the small clippers to trim the fetlocks. However, the heavier hair will dull the blade pretty fast, so it's better to use larger clippers. Be careful using clippers around your horse's feet. Make sure he is accustomed to them. Don't assume because he tolerates clippers around his head that he is automatically happy

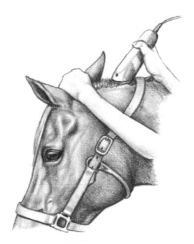

Trim the bridle path to help give your horse a polished look.

Carefully trim the long hair behind his feet, called the fetlocks.

with them buzzing around his feet. Because he can't see much directly below his body without turning his head, he may find the clippers more threatening when they are coming at his feet. He may strike or kick, so position yourself safely. You may even want to pick his legs up to trim them, like you are going to pick out his feet — this way you will have a better idea when he is going to try to move his feet. Again, if he has not been exposed to clippers very often or you are still learning how to use them, have an experienced adult help you the first few times.

The other area to keep clipped is the bridle path behind your horse's ears (where the crownpiece sits). In front of it is the foretop and behind it is the rest of the mane. The bridle path should be around 4 inches long, although you should check your specific discipline; 1 inch is enough for a hunter. You will definitely need larger clippers like the ones you used for the fetlocks to cut the coarse mane hair.

Here's a tip: Decide how far back you want to trim and pull the next couple of inches away in a rubber band. That way you will be less likely to clip too much. After you cut the initial mane hair away, make sure the shaved area is neat and level.

Safe Spraying

All sorts of sprays and gels and creams exist to help detangle your horse's mane and tail and make his coat shiny. These products also repel dust and keep your horse looking spiffy the day of the show. However, be very careful with these products, especially ones that list the ingredient silicone. Don't spray them on the saddle or girth area of the horse – your saddle may be inclined to slip off! Keep a pair of gloves handy for use with these products, and wash your hands after. They can make your hands so slippery you may find it hard to grip the reins.

IMPORTANT: When spraying any sort of product on your horse, don't let him breathe it in, and make sure you don't inhale it either.

Pay special attention to white or light-colored legs because they stain easily.

Lovely Legs

If your horse has white on his legs, use baby powder or cornstarch for temporary whitening to cover up any discolored places and make his socks look nice and white (if you scrub white socks the day before, wrap them to keep them white). Do this before you are dressed in your dark hunt seat outfit. Powder has a way of blowing where you don't want it to, and your navy blue jacket could become speckled pretty quickly. Better yet, have your friend, mom, or "groom" do it — and have a towel handy to wipe down your boots.

Hooves

Don't forget your horse's hooves. Buy your favorite hoof-blackening product and have it handy to apply right before you enter the class, especially a halter class, where appearance is the main focus. Legs with white socks end in white hooves; you don't want to blacken these, but do use a clear polish. You can even buy polishes with a bit of sparkly stuff in them, just for fun!

Show Story

Lyndsey loves grooming her horse. She shows up early before lessons and gives Rowdy a good brushing. Danielle is amazed that Lyndsey always knows the right little tricks to get her horse looking spotless and neat. Danielle wants to know more about grooming too, but just like being a hairstylist, some people have a knack and some don't. She asked Lyndsey if she would give her some lessons. Lyndsey thought if one person was interested in learning more about grooming, maybe others were too.

Lyndsey put up a sign on the barn bulletin board offering one hour of grooming lessons the first Wednesday of every month and charged $5 per person for the lesson. After each lesson, she handed out a list of the grooming tools that her students should have for the next lesson. Everyone loved it. One night they worked on braiding manes and tails. In another lesson, Lyndsey offered tips on getting your horse's coat real shiny. She also taught about making white hair look white, and last-minute grooming tips for showing.

Lyndsey had lots of fun teaching stuff she knew and enjoyed, and to top it off she made enough money to pay for one of her weekly lessons every month!

Braiding

Braids are appropriate for English riders. Both Western and English riders may band the mane, so if you are showing both styles of tack, go ahead and band — you don't want to be braiding and unbraiding at the show! Braid manes and tails as close to the time of the show as possible so they remain neat. Look at the photos throughout this book to learn about the different styles of braiding and when they are appropriate.

Be Patient

Don't be discouraged if the clipping, bathing, and braiding don't go too well the first few times you show your horse. There is a lot of information to remember and many new tasks to learn before you feel proficient. If you are diligent in educating your horse, exposing him carefully to new things, and willing to work hard to master all the skills that go along with riding, you'll soon find that the showing experience goes smoothly every time. Or at least as smoothly as you can ever expect it to!

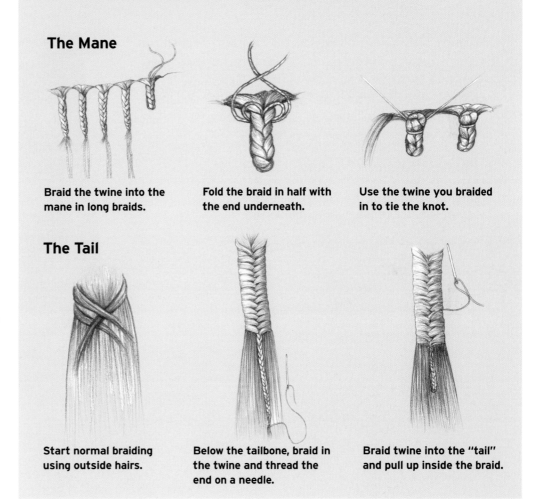

Braiding 101

You need about 30 pieces of twine, each about 12 inches long.

The Mane

Braid the twine into the mane in long braids.

Fold the braid in half with the end underneath.

Use the twine you braided in to tie the knot.

The Tail

Start normal braiding using outside hairs.

Below the tailbone, braid in the twine and thread the end on a needle.

Braid twine into the "tail" and pull up inside the braid.

Grooming Supplies

Following is a list of the things you will need for grooming, in the order that you will need them. Keep this checklist taped to your tack trunk, or copy a few of them to check off for each show. How much time you will need for each depends on how often you show and how dirty your horse is!

❑ Brushes of different firmness

❑ Clippers: small size for whiskers and ears, larger size for bridle path and fetlocks

❑ Small pair of scissors and/or safety razor

❑ Shampoo, wash mitt, scraper, and clean towel

❑ Mane and tail comb with rotating teeth

❑ Mane and tail detangling product

❑ Braiding equipment (comb, bands, twine or yarn, pull-through, scissors, sponge to dampen)

❑ Hoof pick and hoof blackener/polish

❑ Sheet or light blanket

❑ Elbow grease!

PART 3

It's Show Time!

EIGHT

Dressing
for Success

Requirements for what you wear differ depending on what type of showing you want to do, and trends and fashions change over the years. But don't despair; classic looks are always in style. There are ways to find out what the current style is before you spend any money on an outfit. And there are ways to be stylishly turned out for a show without breaking your piggy bank!

Ask your trainer or instructor about current trends in show fashion. You can also watch the big shows on television and look in tack catalogs or visit Web sites that show pictures of winning riders.

Colorful Kids

"I like a more traditional turnout for the English rider. However, kids can get away with adding more splashes of color than adults can. Just don't overdo it."

– Carla Wennberg,
AQHA judge

Safety Equipment

The most important piece of clothing you have is your helmet — never forget it! An ASTM-approved helmet is required by any public show you will attend. In fact, most shows require riders under 18 to have on a helmet every minute that they are mounted. Make sure your chinstrap fits correctly and is fastened at all times. Buy the highest-quality helmet you can — one good helmet is better than two or three mediocre ones.

For smaller shows, you can use your favorite helmet. For regional and upper-level shows, you might want to be more stylish. At the lower levels of competition, even dressage, any helmet is acceptable as long as it meets the safety standards.

A helmet is the most important part of show attire.

All proper riding boots have a significant heel. This helps prevent your entire foot from slipping through the stirrup and causing a dangerous situation where you could be caught by the ankle if you fall off. It is best to buy horse-specific riding boots to wear to a show. They are designed with safety features such as built-in support and just the right size heel. Although your feet may grow out of your boots pretty fast, don't scrimp on them. Think about the fact that in many showing situations your boots are at easy eye level for the judge!

For any high-powered jumping event like cross-country or stadium jumping at the higher levels (protective vests aren't often used for hunter-over-fences classes), you can strap on your protective vest. Don't be shy about protecting yourself. If it feels right, do it!

Western Attire

For most classes, Western riders can wear a nice pair of riding jeans and cowboy boots. Top those off with a cotton blouse and a cowboy hat, and you are in business! You can wear paddock-height boots or lace-up short boots, but be sure your pants are long enough to cover your ankles when you sit in the saddle. Western riders usually buy jeans one or two lengths longer than what they wear for regular old walking-around jeans.

Your cotton blouse can be a simple Oxford-type shirt, the kind that usually comes in white, pale pink, pale blue, or pale yellow. Or you can splurge on some of the real Western high-style shirts with tailoring, piping, and mother-of-pearl snaps. A simple bolo tie, small, neat scarf, or a horsey neck pin is okay, too. The important thing is to look neatly turned out and not too fussy.

Cowboy hats in the show ring tend to be black or white; both go well with any color combination outfit. You can get fancy and have a colored western hat, but in that case you will probably need a different hat for every outfit.

Western riders often wear chaps that are designed for shows, though you can wear regular working chaps

Although an ASTM-certified helmet is the safest thing for your head, Western show style calls for a cowboy hat.

if you compete in working cow and ranch horse classes. Chaps are usually brown or black, but can come in colors. Pleasure class chaps are typically suede, not leather.

Because fringe bounces around, some people think it makes your leg look less steady at the trot. Others think it distracts from a busy leg. If you like fringe, go for it. The length of fringe is also a matter of personal preference and current style.

For a striking Western outfit, make black the predominant color. Your shirt or jacket can have bright pink, turquoise, or bright yellow accents to make an otherwise black outfit look striking. It's easy to match that with black jeans and a black hat. You can also add a splash of color with a bright shirt under a black jacket.

Helmets vs. Hats

Sadly, Western riding has not embraced the use of certified protective headgear. Western riders generally wear cowboy hats in the show ring instead of riding helmets. There have been various attempts at making protective headgear that looks like a Western cowboy hat but has a helmet with an approved safety rating inside the bowl of the hat. The result, unfortunately, is rather large and not very attractive and has not been embraced by Western competitors. We have chosen to include Western riding information in this book, but we do not advocate riding without a helmet.

English Attire

The key with any English-style attire is simplicity and muted tones. Brown saddle and brown bridle, black boots, a dark coat — black, navy blue, dark green, dark gray — tan breeches, a white shirt, and black or brown gloves make any hunter pony and rider look well turned out.

Let your horse shine and attract the judge's eye, not your clothing.

Neutral tones are best in English classes.

Hair, Hair, Everywhere!

If you have short hair, you don't need to worry much about it. If your hair is shoulder length or longer, however, it must be neat. Younger competitors usually wear their hair in braids. When you're older, you can tie it back with a hair elastic or braid it and pin it up. Use a hairnet if you feel it isn't going to stay put. You'll probably need to loosen your helmet strap a little to accommodate a wad of hair in the back. Well before your first show, find what works best for you to keep your hair tidy and out of your way.

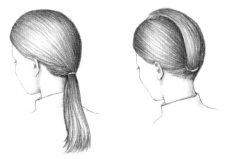

Make a low ponytail, then flip it up and bobby-pin it to the top of your head. Put your helmet on over it.

Dressage Attire

For dressage showing, think black and white. Black coat, black boots, black saddle, black bridle with white trim. White breeches, white shirt, white saddle pad. You can't go wrong with this classic look. You can add a splash of color with a bright lapel pin or small design on your white pad. But the simpler, the better. In a dressage test, you are under individual scrutiny so you do not need anything flashy to call attention to yourself. Gloves are usually optional, but if you wear them, they should be white. And spotless!

In-hand Attire

For in-hand (halter and showmanship) classes, you don't have to wear a helmet or even formal riding attire, although you can. Do, however, wear sturdy shoes appropriate to handling horses. Your horse probably won't step on you, but you just never know. Being stepped on by a thousand-pound animal hurts no matter how it happens. Fancy shoes just don't look appropriate.

For halter classes, you can wear the same type of clothes you would wear riding. Chaps are not necessary. For showmanship, where you have your horse in hand and do a pattern with him, handlers generally dress in a smart outfit, even a suit; you don't want to look like you're headed to the office, but you don't need to wear actual riding clothes, although you can.

Jumping Attire

Your safety helmet is obviously most important in a jumping class. A velvet helmet is the classic jumping helmet: Make sure yours fits well and has a snug-fitting chinstrap or harness. You can place a velvet cover over a regular safety helmet if you wish.

Some jumping competitors also choose to wear a safety vest, which is not a bad idea. Many lightweight styles are readily available.

Again, a dark jacket with riding breeches in tan, black, or even white and tall English boots are the standard. Be sure your jacket fits smartly but loosely enough that you aren't restricted as you go over the jump.

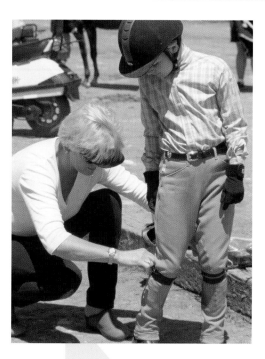

Have a Helper

Every detail of your appearance should show a neat, thoughtful presentation to the judge. It's a good idea to have a friend or family member who can serve as your groom at the show. That person can check you over for loose hair and dangling threads. She should have a clean towel in her pocket to wipe the mud off your boots once you climb on.

Show Story

Working hunter classes had been loads of fun for Jory. This was her third season showing on the regional level. But her horse, Thud, was getting a little bored with it. She knew he had more in him; in fact, she had jumped him lots

higher than the jumps typical of the hunter-over-saddle height.

Jory used her journal to explore what she might want to do next. She found she could think things through a lot better if she wrote her thoughts down. She attended a couple of dressage shows to watch. It just all seemed too stuffy and slow to a 15- (almost 16!) year-old. She even checked out some Western classes, but that would require a huge change and she didn't see Thud as a Western-style horse or herself as a Western-style rider. In the end, Jory decided that she really did love jumping and she wanted to stick with it. But she also decided she was going to head for stadium jumping events — higher fences and higher competition. Jory was a hard worker and good competitor and knew she could give it a run.

It was nice, too, that she really wouldn't need much different equipment. She had a high-quality jumping saddle and breeches and coats in a myriad of colors. The one thing she decided to buy new was a top-of-the-line titanium helmet. The most she had ever spent on a helmet was just under $100; titanium ones ran almost $300. But she knew that higher fences meant farther to fall and she did plan to go to college and thought she might need her head for that! So Jory took on a few extra babysitting jobs and did some minor bookkeeping for her aunt to save up the money, bought the helmet right after school started, and planned to begin her show jumping training just after the end of this year's show season.

Buying Used

One of the hardest parts about buying riding clothes if you're a kid is that you don't stay the same size for very long. This is where used show clothes come in handy.

You can find used-tack shops in almost any part of the country, where you can look for riding clothes. Show clothes often stay in good condition because they are not used hard like your everyday riding clothes.

Buying used also allows you to buy good quality. And high-quality clothing will stay in better shape, have a longer life, and be easier to sell once you are done with it.

Your used-tack shop will probably have all of the show clothing separated into different disciplines. What you would wear for saddle seat riding, for example, is not the same as what you would wear for hunter/jumper performances.

One last thing about buying used: Buy only very traditional, classic clothes. Anything flashy is probably already out of style. Look in equestrian catalogs to see what clothes are currently in fashion so you can avoid buying used items that are hopelessly outdated.

You can also buy used boots, but it may take some searching to find the right size. As well as used-tack shops, try searching for boots on eBay.

Foul Weather

Don't forget to pack your foul-weather gear. The show will go on rain or shine even if it is being held outdoors. You will want a clear rain jacket and perhaps even pants for yourself. It won't look as nice as if you weren't wearing them, but it certainly looks better than being soaked to the skin. And it feels better too!

Bring a rain cover for your saddle at least, and preferably a rain sheet that fits over your saddle while covering much of your horse. (Of course, you should make sure your horse is comfortable with a flapping rain sheet by introducing him to it long before show time.) You should also have a rain cover for your helmet — if it's velvet, it will protect it, and if it isn't, it will prevent rain from dripping in the ventilation holes.

Rubbers will protect your boots from mud and rain, keep your feet more comfortable, and can even be helpful on sunny days to protect your boots from dust.

A Horse of a Different Color

Some of your tack and clothing decisions will be based on the color of your horse. A gray looks great carrying black clothing and tack with a splash of color to liven up the look. A chestnut horse looks more natural with brown tack, and perhaps a touch of green or blue. A bay, perhaps the most common color of all, has the best of both worlds — either black or brown matches, and red is a nice accent color.

Color Wheel

Just as people look better in certain colors, so do horses. This chart is for Western competitors. Find your horse's color in the inner (white) circles. Then look at the colors on the rim of the "wheel" right next to the horse color. These will be the best shades for you to wear to complement your horse's coat.

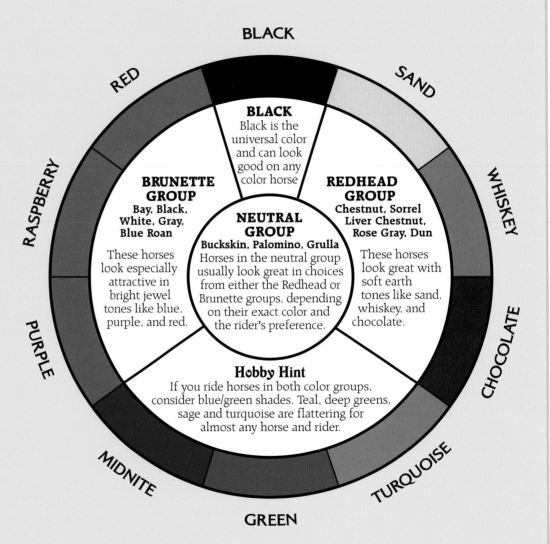

BLACK

RED

SAND

RASPBERRY

WHISKEY

PURPLE

CHOCOLATE

MIDNITE

TURQUOISE

GREEN

BLACK
Black is the universal color and can look good on any color horse

BRUNETTE GROUP
Bay, Black, White, Gray, Blue Roan

These horses look especially attractive in bright jewel tones like blue, purple, and red.

NEUTRAL GROUP
Buckskin, Palomino, Grulla
Horses in the neutral group usually look great in choices from either the Redhead or Brunette groups, depending on their exact color and the rider's preference.

REDHEAD GROUP
Chestnut, Sorrel Liver Chestnut, Rose Gray, Dun

These horses look great with soft earth tones like sand, whiskey, and chocolate.

Hobby Hint
If you ride horses in both color groups, consider blue/green shades. Teal, deep greens, sage and turquoise are flattering for almost any horse and rider.

The Final Check

Before you go into the ring, have a show buddy – a friend, your mom, a fellow competitor – give you the once-over to check for anything that has gone astray. Look for:

"Don'ts"

◆ Hair falling out of the back of your helmet.

◆ Helmet straps flying in the breeze.

◆ Mud or dirt on your boots. (Keep a towel handy for quick wipe-ups.)

◆ Mud or dirt on your horse's legs (as much as it can be helped).

◆ Untied boot lacings.

◆ Unbuttoned buttons on your jacket or shirt.

◆ Anything that looks unkempt, loose, or out of place.

"Dos"

◆ A clearly visible "pin" or number on the back of your jacket.

◆ Shirttails neatly tucked into your pants or breeches.

◆ Buttons done up in the right order.

◆ Helmet on straight – there's nothing that can quickly make you look crooked more than a crooked helmet!

NINE

Planning
for a Show

You've got a show coming up. Oh my! What do you do first?

At the back of this book, you will find a series of checklists that will help you organize everything you need (and there is a lot to remember!). There are five main parts to every show experience. The first is to register, preferably well in advance. The second is preparing your horse (grooming, cleaning tack, braiding manes, and so on). The third is preparing yourself (show clothes, eating a good breakfast, staying calm, and so on). The fourth is the show itself. And the fifth is cleaning up afterward so that you'll be ahead of the game for the next show!

Take the High Road

"Competition can do odd things to people. In order to win, some exhibitors lose sight of good horsemanship and sportsmanship. In the desperate dash for the blue ribbon, they sometimes treat horses inhumanely and fellow exhibitors discourteously. I hope this won't happen to you. There are many routes to the winners' circle, but often the slower you go, the faster you'll get there!"

— Cherry Hill, *trainer, author, and longtime judge*

Check, and Check Again!

Use the checklists at the back of this book as you prepare for each show. If you show with your riding academy or lesson barn, create a set of checklists for the trailer there. They will love you for it!

Planning Is the Key

Planning your show season and each individual show day is the key to having a successful show career. You can't just throw things in a bag at the last minute, load up your horse, head for the show, and expect to win your classes. Take whatever time you need to prepare for your classes, plan for the day, and plan for the season. You may need more preparation time than your friend does, and that's okay. If you need a lot less, that's okay too. Just be sure you aren't doing things in a rush. Relax and enjoy yourself!

Registering

Once you decide which shows you want to attend, contact the sponsoring organization for registration information. If you are on its regular mailing list, you will receive flyers and other info through the mail soliciting your participation. These mailings should tell you everything you need to know — for instance, if a stable sponsors several dressage events over the season, it may send you a list of them all, with the opening and closing dates for registration for each. Registering in advance allows the sponsoring organization to better plan for the number of participants. This helps keep costs down and in turn helps membership dues stay as low as possible.

Find out if you need to send in copies of your horse's negative results from a Coggins test and proof of rabies vaccine and any other vaccination history it may require. Often you need to send a check made out to the organization with no amount filled in and it will figure out your total and send it back to you with your registration verification.

The Day Before

Organize all your clothing at least a day in advance (both your show attire and any other clothes you'll need). Put items that can wrinkle on hangers. If you have more than one show outfit, lay out each one on your bed the night before. Include boots, socks, and every little detail for the entire outfit, right down to your hairpins. That way you know you have everything. Don't leave this important task to your mom. She may be able to help, but it's your responsibility to have everything you need packed up and ready to go. Once you have everything laid out, pack it neatly in your suitcase or garment bag. Put small items like hairpins and stock brooches together in a zipped bag.

Now go through the same routine for your horse. Lay out everything ahead of time: tack (clean, of course!), leg wraps, grooming kit, first-aid kit, etc. Make sure you know where everything is in your travel trunk and that all the supplies are restocked (fly spray, mane detangler, etc.). Put as much as you can in the trailer the night before you leave.

See the checklists at the end of this book for suggestions on what to take.

Visualizing

As you are preparing and packing, imagine your performance in your head. This is called "visualization." Visualize success! Picture yourself and your horse doing your best.

Staying Safe

Planning is also the key to safety. For example, try to arrive at each show in a calm frame of mind ready to take on any challenge thrown your way. Rushing around, sending in forms at the last minute, and getting to the show 20 minutes before your first class is a good way to forget things and jeopardize your and your horse's safety. Be prepared, be early, be calm, and you'll also be in control and practicing good safety!

Spend some quiet time picturing yourself at the show, staying centered and calm.

Sweet Dreams

After you are sure everything is organized and ready, go to bed. That's no joke — a good night's rest is crucial for competing at your optimum level. Showing takes a lot of energy, both mental and physical. Your horse deserves 100 percent consistency from you in the show environment. You've spent all this money and all this time and you want to give it your best try, right? Right! Then go to bed early. You will sleep better knowing you have everything organized and ready for takeoff in the morning. Drift off dreaming good thoughts about your winning round at the show.

Early to Rise . . .

Wait! Before you lay your head on the pillow, set the alarm for earlier than you think you might need to get up. Leave plenty of time to have some breakfast. If you feel too anxious to eat, fix your favorite breakfast so you will be tempted to eat. Bring some extra snacks for the road, too. You need the energy from a good break-

A good night's sleep will help you do your best.

fast to think clearly, stay calm, and compete at your best.

Getting up early will also allow you plenty of time to do all sorts of last-minute tasks. Being relaxed and not hurrying will help your horse stay calm as well. Horses seem to know when people are in a rush, and they have a way of throwing a wrench into the works. If you are in a hurry, they tend to decide that today isn't such a good day to load into the trailer. Or while you are standing in back of the trailer anxiously waiting for your dad to put the ramp down, your horse will slobber green goo all over your clean ratcatcher, which you already put on because you are in the first class of the day. Or he will step on your toes so that you take up some precious time hopping around saying ouch for ten minutes. Horses just know when we are hurrying and they just seem to know that hurrying is not a good thing.

Centering Yourself

Remember, horse showing is supposed to be at least partly fun! One key to having fun is not to feel rushed and anxious about whether you'll be on time, you have everything you need, or you've pinned your hair up securely enough. A little extra time up front means you can enjoy the adrenaline rush of entering the show ring knowing that every hair is in place.

Each time it gets easier. Before long you'll have a smooth and effortless routine.

Show Story

What happens when you don't get ready ahead of time for a show? Rachel knew all too well that being disorganized before the show meant being disorganized at the show too.

She used to just explain it away as being a "free spirit." That being so organized, like Susie is, was just too boring for her. She'd been to enough shows by now, after all, to know what she needed and could just throw it together that morning. Of course, she really didn't like to get up early, so that sounded okay in theory.

Rachel had to change something when she began to go to bigger shows and teamed up with three other girls at her lesson barn. They all rode in Courtney's mom's four-horse trailer and huge truck. But after the third show, Courtney and the other two girls told Rachel that if she didn't get more organized, she wouldn't be able to go with them. They often had to wait for Rachel to show up at the barn. Not only would they all be ready to go, but they had also done all of Rachel's chores too, so they wouldn't have to wait for her to do them when she finally showed up. And when they got to the show, Rachel was always borrowing stuff from them. It wasn't that she didn't have her own; it was all sitting back at the barn because she forgot it.

Rachel understood. But she didn't know how to get more organized. She thought she didn't want to, but in fact it had been bothering her. She and her horse did okay, but she felt that if she were more together, she would be able to be more successful in the ring too. And she was sure her horse picked up on her rushing around trying to make up for lost time.

Her three friends wanted to have Rachel along – they liked her and she was so funny. So they started to help her get more organized. First, they pitched in and bought Rachel an alarm clock and preset it to 5:30 A.M. to help her get off on a better foot. They helped her make up some checklists that would help her organize her stuff. And they bribed her with food and fun if she started pulling stuff together, cleaning tack, and packing what she could earlier in the week before the show. She even began to arrive in time to get the horses loaded in the trailer.

Rachel not only was thrilled to be able to stick with her friends, but she also found she and her horse began to place a little more frequently in their classes. Being a little organized, she decided, wasn't so boring after all.

At the Show

Make sure your parents know what time you need to be at the show or at the barn to leave for the show. Arrive on the show grounds with plenty of time to spare before your first class. If you've booked a stall in the show barn, get your horse settled. If it's just a day show, you may leave him in the trailer or tie him to the side, but always leave a person with the trailer in case your horse gets in trouble. Then head for the secretary's booth or table. This is "command central," where you will find out everything you need to know to plan the logistics for your day.

Your Horse Comes First

Take care of your horse before all else. He relies on you to make sure he is comfortable and healthy at the show. If you have to run to the bathroom, ask someone to stand at the trailer with him. If you have a stall on the show grounds, unload your horse and settle him in his stall as soon as possible. Fill your horse's water bucket and hay bag before you go have your own lunch. The show isn't your horse's idea (or his idea of fun!), so be sure to attend to his needs in exchange for his participation.

Getting Your Bearings

If you have preregistered (and for all but the smallest local shows, this is crucial), you can just check in at the secretary's booth, pick up your number and the class list, and start studying what your day will look like. If you still need to register for classes, find the list and select your classes. While you're at the secretary's booth, take care of the following details.

◆ If you have back-to-back classes in different disciplines and have to change tack in between, request a "tack change" hold between those classes.

◆ Find out when showmanship, trail, jumping, and equitation patterns will be posted.

◆ Ask when the lunch break will be. Some huge shows don't have one; they just keep moving along and you take lunch whenever you have time between classes. You can use a lunch break for lots of things besides lunch — warm up in the practice ring, check the braids in your horse's mane, find your friend to borrow a hair band; you name it.

◆ Find out what is taking place where. Even some of the smallest shows have different rings for pleasure classes and trail or jumping classes. This allows the jumps and obstacles to remain set up while the rest of the show keeps going on.

◆ Locate the bathrooms! You don't want to be looking around for these when you really need one.

Once you get into showing, you will probably go to the same shows and show grounds year after year. You will know where everything is and your list of settling-in tasks will be a lot shorter. But until then, take the time to make your new showing experience a good one.

Top Causes of Show Accidents

Here are some situations and habits to avoid.

1. Letting your horse come too close to other horses either inside or outside the show ring.

2. Not preparing your horse properly for the horse show atmosphere.

3. Hanging around at show ring entrance and exit gates, either on foot or on your horse.

4. Poor maintenance of your tack.

5. Ignoring show grounds safety precautions and rules.

6. Reckless behavior such as cantering your horse anywhere except designated warm-up areas or riding your horse in places that are off-limits.

7. Leaving unsupervised horses tied to the trailer.

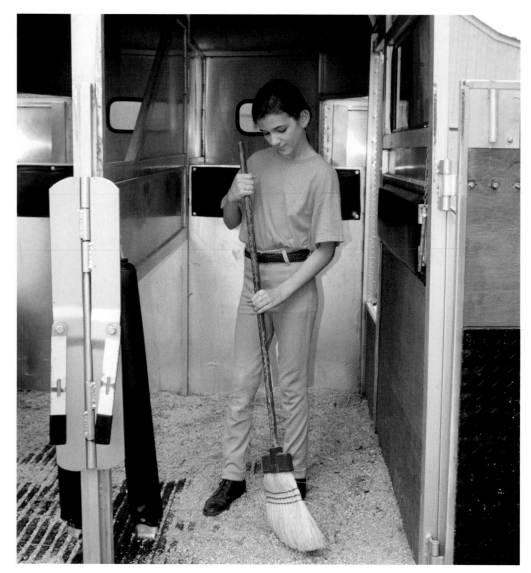
Being organized and neat is a very important aspect of show success.

Food

Most shows, large and small, have a food booth. The food at these booths has gotten a little healthier over the years. Although doughnuts are often the main breakfast fare and cheeseburgers and hotdogs are the main lunch entrée, sandwich wraps and salads appear on many menus. If you are picky about food or prefer to eat more healthfully, bring along some food of your own. Nutritious snacks like fruit and small puddings are ideal pick-me-ups when you have some free time. Remember, healthy food will keep your energy level up and your brain working at its best.

The same goes for drinks. Bring along a cooler with bottles of water, soft drinks, and juices. You can get pretty thirsty, and it's much easier to grab a soda out of your trailer than to run to the food booth — especially when you get there and realize you don't have money in your breeches! Make things easy for yourself. Bring enough to offer a soda or snack to a riding pal or two. They'll undoubtedly return the favor someday!

Good Sportsmanship

Here are some tried-and-true guidelines for being a good sport and a respected competitor.

◆ Never approach the judge without permission. If you do have a specific question, ask the ring steward or the announcer or another official if you may speak to the judge.

◆ Always be gracious, whether you won the blue ribbon or didn't place at all. Leave the ring politely and smiling, and kindly pat your horse for trying. If it was a show you worked very hard to prepare for and you missed the championship by just a couple of points, go ahead and shed a few tears in the privacy of your trailer. But make it quick, because there's plenty of work to be done!

◆ Always congratulate the winners if you have the opportunity. Be enthusiastic about the success of the other riders you came to the show with, even if it hasn't been your day (and even if you don't like a particular person very much). When other competitors treat you this way, you'll know why it's important.

◆ Learn how to salute the judge for your dressage test. If you carry a whip, don't slap the whip up in the air with your salute; that looks kind of silly! Although trends do change, the standard salute is to drop your head slightly and extend your arm straight down.

◆ Know the rules of the sponsoring association of any show circuit you participate in. For instance, did you know that "braiding the mane or tail is not permitted for Pony Club events, except for Dressage competitions at the upper levels"? This rule appears in *The United States Pony Club Manual of Horsemanship: Basics for Beginners, D Level.* It's fairly easy to obtain the rules of most organizations just by requesting their rule book through either e-mail or snail mail.

◆ If your horse refuses a jump, know whether the rules of the show allow you to take a "courtesy jump." Insurance regulations have changed these rules over the years — some show circuits consider it a liability to let a competitor try the jump again if her horse refused the first time.

◆ Sometimes your horse may be hard to handle in a class. If you feel that he's out of control, ask the ring steward to excuse you from the class. Either you will sit out the class in the middle of the ring or you will be assisted in exiting the gate at an appropriate time.

TEN

On the
Big Day

Showing horses is all about competition. Yes, you have fun. You enjoy being with your horse and doing something different. And you learn a lot, too. But ultimately, your intention is to win ribbons. Ribbons are your "grades," a benchmark that shows how you and your horse are doing compared to others at your level of education.

But you aren't always going to win. Even when you've worked really hard to prepare. Even when you feel that you and your pony had the best class you've ever had together. Here are some important things to remember about the entire showing experience that will make it more fun for you — even when you don't go home with the blue.

Be Positive

"Judges are human. If a rider has a positive look and I can tell she wants to win and has done her homework, I'm a cheerleader for her all day. But the opposite can happen, too — if a rider is always jerking on her horse, has a sour look, and seems unhappy with herself and her horse, so am I."

— **Carla Wennberg,**
AQHA judge

The Ups and Downs of Showing

Showing, like all things in life that we work hard at, has its ups and downs, its joys and frustrations. If you learn to take both the wins and the losses with grace, you will earn the reputation of being a great competitor.

A Winning Mental Attitude

It's important for you to concentrate on doing your best, no matter what situation you're in. Every class you enter, after all, contains a different group of competitors, and every class is judged by a certain set of criteria. The horse and rider team that best meets those criteria should win the class. But in subjectively judged classes (see page 18), you are being compared to the other teams. So a blue-ribbon performance in one class may not be a winning performance in a class with a different group of competitors.

Dealing with Nerves

The first time you ride in a class at a show, you will almost certainly be

This is the moment you've been working for for so long.

nervous. That's okay! Nerves can help you focus. If you think you are way too nervous — as if your knees would be knocking together if there weren't a horse between them — then here are some ways to calm down a little.

◆ Breathe deeply.

◆ Think about being in your practice ring at home.

◆ Say to yourself: "I am relaxed." Sometimes all it takes to start to feel something is to say it aloud.

◆ Visualize all those good rides you've had.

◆ Let your horse help calm you. Give her a big warm hug and a kiss on that soft muzzle before your first class. If she is a show veteran, she can really help you survive the first few classes. This is one excellent reason for a beginner to have a horse to show that knows the ropes better than she does.

David O'Connor:
Equestrian of the Year

David O'Connor, a world-class equestrian who has set records and excelled at the Olympics in both individual and team competition, was named Equestrian of the Year for 2002 by the United States Equestrian Federation. The award is given to an athlete who has "excelled above all others in equestrian competition for the current year, while demonstrating superior sportsmanship and dedication to the principles, vision, and mission of USEF." Good sportsmanship is valued even among the top riders in the world!

Frustration: It's Inevitable

You will feel frustrated sometimes in your show career. It's not that you *get* frustrated but *how you handle it* that will count.

Most important, don't take your frustration out on your horse. He is doing what he thinks you are asking him to do. If he is simply behaving badly, your job is to teach him — long before the show — that misbehaving is unacceptable. He doesn't know this on his own; he is doing what comes naturally to a horse in a given situation.

Overcoming Performance Jitters

Almost everyone, even top-level competitors, has experienced performance jitters. Some competitors who have been on the scene for a while admit that they still feel anxious before entering the show ring. The important thing is to learn how to relax under stress.

The best way to overcome your fears is to have confidence in yourself. You know that you and your pony can do this class perfectly – you have trained and practiced over and over. Now it's time to focus on your performance and forget about the spectators, the other competitors, and any other factors that may make you nervous.

Waiting for your turn in the show ring can be an anxious time.

Figure out what is causing your frustration. Is it because the same competitor keeps winning in the classes you enter? Don't waste energy fretting over something you can't change. Ask a friend to watch your classes and see what the winning team is doing better. Or consider sitting out a class, or even a whole show, and learn for yourself what makes her performance more effective than yours. Then start practicing!

Ribbon Colors

In U.S. competition, colored ribbons are given for the following places.

first: blue
second: red
third: yellow
fourth: white
fifth: pink
sixth: green
seventh: purple
eighth: brown
ninth: dark gray
tenth: light blue

Don't Take Gossip to Heart

If you go to enough horse shows, you will hear gossip and rumors about other competitors, judges, horses, trainers; you name it. Make an agreement with yourself to forget gossip as soon as you've heard it. Do not let it affect your performance or show experience. Above all, never repeat gossip. To do so is bad form in all aspects of life, and it is definitely bad sportsmanship. Remember, gossip is often not even true; it is just one person's opinion or perspective.

Be Ready for Anything

Even though you spend many hours practicing and preparing for a show, there are some things you just can't anticipate. Your horse throws a shoe, you forget your saddle, or you get sick the day before or, worse, at the show.

Go with it. Be as prepared as possible and do the best you can with the unexpected.
And try to learn from the surprises so you can prevent them from occurring next time.

Expect the unexpected
at a horse show!

Show Ring Etiquette

Most young riders have someone "on the rail" who has helped them train for their show performance. This person might be a coach, a trainer, or a riding instructor. Most are helpful but some are not.

Here are some suggestions on making sure your support team is truly supportive.

A good coach will school you outside the ring and leave you alone while you are performing.

Trainers on the Rail

Your coach should be there for you and should help you tweak things to give your best performance. But avoid a coach who stands at the rail barking orders at you while you are riding in a class. This can be distracting. A quiet "Sit up straight" or "Look up" as you pass can be helpful if you are a green show rider. But this is not the time for the coach to be schooling you and your horse. If your coach is grumpy and bossy while you are in the ring, try talking with her about it. If she is not receptive to your concerns, find someone else.

Parents on the Rail

The same goes for your mom or dad. It can be hard to tell your parents to leave you alone in the ring. Let them know that you appreciate their support and are happy that they care about your equine endeavors enough to spend their weekends at horse shows. But it won't help you win a class if your mom stands on the sidelines giving you instructions, especially if she doesn't ride herself!

Show Story

If Courtney won the Western pleasure class one more time, Elaine was going to burst with frustration. Elaine always pinned second or third, but every time Courtney was in the class — which was *every* time — Courtney and her beautiful Paint horse, Bleu (yes, the French spelling of Blue, of course), won the blue. It was sickening. Elaine practiced and practiced, had started with a new instructor, and still couldn't come out ahead of Courtney.

This had been going on for it seems as long as Elaine could remember. And every show, and every year, Elaine got more and more frustrated with it, enough so that she now did not even speak to Courtney. That bothered her, but she couldn't help herself. And Courtney had stopped speaking to her too,

although for a long time she attempted to be friends. How could you be friends, thought Elaine, with someone who beats you all the time?

Elaine began to dislike showing, and it showed. Her mother would growl at her from the rail to smile and at least *look* as if she were having fun. Once more, Courtney won the blue. Elaine got third.

Elaine decided enough was enough. She didn't like feeling this way, or that her inner feelings were affecting her performance. Finally, after one class, she rode over to Courtney's trailer and congratulated her on her win. Courtney seemed genuinely surprised and pleased.

After that, Courtney and Elaine started to chat more often. Elaine asked Courtney some questions about her schooling work. Elaine

even sat out a couple of classes and watched Courtney carefully. When she won, as usual, Elaine found herself clapping enthusiastically. Courtney and Bleu really were a pleasure to watch.

Elaine started making some changes to her own performance. At show, Courtney couldn't ride because she was recovering from a bad case of the flu. And Elaine won the Western pleasure class! Courtney now clapped enthusiastically from the stands. The real test was two shows later, when finally, at long last, Elaine won and Courtney came in second. Courtney was so excited, you'd think she herself had won. Elaine couldn't help think what sportsmanship that showed on Courtney's part. And they've been good friends ever since.

Looking Good

Carla Wennberg is an American Quarter Horse Association (AQHA) and National Reining Horse Association (NRHA) judge. She has judged the AQHA Open and Amateur World Shows, the European Nationals, the Quarter Horse Congress, and the Quarter Horse Youth World Show. To catch her eye, you need to consider the following five things:

1. **Respect for your horse.** How you feel about your horse, Carla says, will show in your attitude during the class or event. A judge wants to see that you respect your horse and appreciate the effort your horse is giving you.

2. **Professional turnout.** This applies to both you and your horse. Wear clothes that fit. Avoid extreme colors. Your horse's equipment should fit properly and be clean and polished. Grooming is important. Braid manes and tails properly and clip correctly.

3. **Invisible aids.** This also relates to doing your homework. You and your horse should have practiced so much that you are completely in tune with each other. This shows the judge that you have worked hard and that you love what you are doing.

4. **Confidence and planning ahead.** This comes with experience, but until you gain a lot of experience, practice, practice, practice. Do your homework and know how to show in the classes you choose to enter. Memorize patterns and tests and arrive at each class on time and ready to ride.

5. **An appropriate match between horse and rider.** This doesn't mean a young rider must ride a pony. But if you are petite, a slender 15.2-hand Thoroughbred may be more suitable for you than a 17.1-hand Hanoverian. Also, you must be able to handle your horse competently, and not have your hands too full.

All of this adds up to one of the most important things to a judge: the first impression.

When you enter the show ring with a smile on your face, you give the impression you are planning to have fun. Your confidence in your horse spills over and you are a pleasure to watch. When your clothes are well chosen, neat, and fit perfectly, the judge will notice you. Your long practice sessions will shine through and the judge will understand that you are prepared and deserve to win.

Find a way to let your parents know if they are making it more difficult for you. Enlist the help of your coach, trainer, or riding instructor if you need to. Maybe your coach could engage your mom in a conversation while they watch you in a class. You want to see your parents on the rail looking proud of you and inspiring you to give it your all. If it doesn't result in a ribbon, so be it. What fun you had anyway!

Winning Ways

The moment is finally here, and you're in the ring. What are the most important things to think about?

Above all, maintain good communication with your horse. You are partners, and you must convince him that you are confident and centered. This will not only help him relax, but it will make your performance shine.

Listen carefully and respond promptly to every instruction given by the judge or other show officials.

Be calm and courteous to the other competitors throughout the class.

Remember to smile!

Be modest if you win — and give your horse a big hug. Be gracious if you don't win — and give your horse an even bigger hug.

Enjoy yourself — this is what you've worked for, for so long!

Reviewing Your Performance

You should always go back over your performance at the show. It's best to do this after you exit each class, but that will depend on how much time you have before your next class.

If your trainer or instructor is with you at the show, she will help you review your class. The more you think about what went right and what went wrong, the more you can improve your performance the next time. It's important to work on your weaknesses, but don't forget to be proud of the things you did well. There's always another chance to do better.

Quiet confidence is like having your very own spotlight.

Ask Yourself

Before a show, make several copies of the opposite page. Write about each class as soon after it as you can.

When you left the exit gate, was the smile on your face real or did you have to force it? If it was genuine, why were you smiling? Maybe it was because you won the blue ribbon! Maybe it was because you won your first ribbon ever. Or maybe you rode really well, even though you didn't place.

What did you do best? This might be something specific, like flying over that line of three jumps as if they weren't even there, or something general. Perhaps your horse responded smoothly to your aids and you just had a great ride. Focus on the best aspects of a class and think about why they were good and how you can repeat them.

What could have gone better? Again, this could be something very specific, like you had to try twice to pick up your right lead canter. Maybe it's something general – your horse was distracted by the crowd and you couldn't get him to pay attention to you. Jot down some specific ways in which you might improve.

Did your horse seem to enjoy himself? How can you tell? Of course, a primary indication is his overall behavior. If he's prancing around or bucking or otherwise acting out, he definitely is not happy with the situation! But there are more subtle things as well. Does he listen to you and wait for your commands or does he simply react to what all the other horses are doing? Is he calm and organized in the trail class or does he have to be reminded what to do at every obstacle? Can you hear his tail swishing madly behind him every time you give him a signal to change gaits?

Learn the signs of frustration and figure out how to change his thinking. Maybe you aren't preparing him enough for the classes you are taking him in. Sometimes it helps to bring him to a couple of shows and not enter any classes. Or enter one class in the morning and one in the afternoon instead of six in the morning and four in the afternoon. Think about whether the discipline you have chosen for your horse is the best one for him – you might find that he makes a great trail horse but pleasure classes bore him to death. Ultimately, he should be able to hold it together for a 15-minute class. But all depends on the horse, your abilities, and your showing experience.

The main thing is, don't just leave a class and rush to the snack bar to chat with your friends until the next class. If you take showing seriously, you owe it to yourself and your horse to review your performance and try to improve upon it each time.

How Did You Do?

Did you enjoy this class?

_____

_____

_____

_____

_____

What could have gone better?

_____

_____

_____

_____

_____

What did you do best in the class?

_____

_____

_____

_____

Did your horse seem to enjoy the class?

_____

_____

_____

_____

ELEVEN

After *the* Show

The show is over. It may have been a long day in the hot sun or a chilly drizzle. Or perhaps the weather was absolutely perfect with a mix of sun and clouds, moderate temperature, and no bugs. Either way, you are mentally and physically tired and ready to go home.

As always, take care of your horse first. Clear out manure and dropped hay in the trailer. Put leg wraps on your horse if you use them and a sheet if you feel it's necessary. Hang a fresh bag of hay. Offer him a drink before he settles into the trailer. Once you have your horse ready for the trip home, pack up your equipment.

The Hardest Part

"I tell my kids: Leave the ring with a smile on your face, make a beeline to the trailer smiling all the way, and then find a way to let out your frustration. Just don't take it out on your horse."

— Joanne Gelinas Snow, *riding instructor & show coach, Pembroke, N.H.*

Tidy Up

Clean up all around your trailer. Don't just wipe loose hay off the bumper or shake the remnants of the hay bag onto the ground; put them in the wheelbarrow for the manure pile. And speaking of manure, scoop that up around the area too. Check for empty soda bottles or candy wrappers lying around and pick them up even if they aren't yours. If you brought lawn chairs, collect them. Leave your parking area neat and tidy so the show management looks forward to you coming back to the next show.

Did you use a stall in the show's barn for the day or the weekend? Return it to the condition it was in when you arrived. Check with the show manager to see if you should refill the stall with fresh shavings. (Some barns want you to do that; others like to let the stalls air out between shows and will replace the shavings themselves.) Pick up all of your trash from the aisle and carry it out with you (always stash an empty grain bag in your trailer; it makes a great trash can).

Take Time to Be a Spectator

If your last class is in the middle of the afternoon, try to stay awhile longer and watch other classes. Now that your classes are over and your nerves have settled, you can relax and learn. You can still benefit even if the classes are not ones that you would choose to enter.

You will learn a lot by observing other competitors in any discipline. Watch them before they go into the ring. How do they calm their nerves? Maybe one rider has a great idea for holding her hair in place that you can use. And it's great sportsmanship to sit on the sidelines and cheer other competitors on and clap for their winnings, even if you don't know who they are!

Heading Out

Say good-bye to your show friends and congratulate them one more time on their performance. You will see the same competitors time and time again at the shows you attend, and it is much more pleasant to be friends with them than to consider them adversaries. You all want the same

Watching other competitors perform is one of the best ways to learn.

thing — to win! — but only one person can win any given class. Accept that, congratulate the winner, and go home determined to do better next time.

Try to thank the show officials. The secretary works hard all day and would appreciate a big smile and a

Teamwork Tip

Teamwork is an important part of showing with a group from your lesson barn. Teamwork skills will help you in all parts of your life, now and in the future — and might even make things at home go more smoothly with your brothers and sisters!

Always do your part. If you are assigned a task you don't understand, ask someone how to do it. Likewise, if a task makes you uncomfortable, it's better to say so. Maybe you can switch with someone. Some chores are not pleasant, but they all must be completed. Take turns switching around your responsibilities so that one person doesn't get stuck with the least popular job all the time.

thank-you for her help processing your forms. The show manager is as exhausted as you are and she didn't even compete! Again, a smile and a thank-you go a long way. It is harder and harder for riding clubs to find volunteer show personnel, so help make sure they know that their efforts are appreciated.

After a long, tiring day, you are probably eager to start for home. But don't hurry out of the parking area. Leave the show grounds as carefully as you entered. Help whoever is driving your rig to see people and horses walking around. If someone is having trouble loading a horse, you probably don't have to stop and help but don't just fly by tossing mud on them! You will see these people again and how you leave them will be the lasting impression.

On the drive home you'll be full of what happened at the show. If you're with a group, you'll also hear the details of your friends' day. Jot down your memories, while they're still fresh, on page 128 — and get your friends' autographs while you're at it!

Celebrate the moment with your show friends before heading down the road.

Horse Show Lingo

Horse shows have their own special language. You may have heard the following words or phrases:

Flat class. Walk, trot, canter in front of a judge.

In the hole. Refers to the rider waiting after the rider who is on deck (see below).

On deck. Refers to the rider waiting to enter the course after the current rider finishes.

Rider up. Refers to a rider who is mounted and ready to go.

Scratch. To withdraw from a class before it is called.

Trip. One completion of a course over fences.

Turnout. Overall appearance of a horse and rider.

Way of going. Overall movement of a horse.

Show Story

The four girls from Rocking Horse Stable cleaned out the trailer first thing at the show, after they put their horses in stalls and before they needed to get their show clothes on. Their coach (who was also their instructor and had trained a couple of their horses) was kind of a drill sergeant about it, but insisted that they do these things before they were all tired and cranky at the end of a long day or weekend.

Whoever finished her last class first began organizing their gear, putting away anything they were not going to need for the rest of the show. Each girl had a list on the back of the tack room door that told what her chores were for the weekend. Each girl knew all the chores. If she finished hers, she started on the others unless there was an important class she should watch.

All of this work paid off, because at the end of the show everything was neat and orderly and ready for departure. It was really a team effort. Despite the fact that sometimes they teased their coach, calling her a military commander, they appreciated being so organized, especially when they parked near other people who were running around frazzled at the end of the show.

They had plenty of time to take pictures of themselves with their ribbons, to watch other classes, and to enjoy the final moments of the show. And they all felt good about contributing to a fun day.

Ask Yourself

At the end of the show, maybe on the ride home, take time to review the entire day. Answer these questions:

How do you feel about the day overall?

_____

_____

Did you enter the right number of classes?

_____

_____

How did your horse act by the end of the day? Did he grow more anxious? More relaxed?

_____

_____

Was the show well organized? Was it well attended? Would you return to this show next year?

_____

_____

Here are some questions to consider with your trainer or instructor:

Did you practice enough at home for the level of the classes you entered?

_____

_____

_____

Were you well organized for the show?

_____

_____

If you were with a group from your lesson barn, did everyone work well as a team? Did everyone know what she was responsible for and do it? Were there any areas that could use improvement next time?

_____

_____

PART 4

What's Next?

TWELVE

Onward
and Upward

How do you know when it's time to move up a stage in your show career? One sure indication is if you are winning almost every class you enter. That may be fun for a while, but it shows that you are ready to move up to something more challenging.

Maybe you are bored with the whole show scene. For several years, you have traveled to the same shows and met the same competitors. You've even had the same things for lunch at the snack bar!

It's time to spark things up a bit. A new show circuit could be just what you need.

Take It Slow

"Don't make big changes across the board. For instance, if you have been showing 3' fences at C-rated shows and decide to move up this year to a B-rated circuit, go back to 2'6" fences. Once you've gained your confidence in a more competitive circuit, you can return to 3' fences. Sometimes it takes a couple of steps backwards to move ahead."

– Lowell Murray,
judge and trainer

To the Next Level

There are a couple of ways to move up. You can advance in your current discipline by entering the next level of competition. For instance, in dressage, there is always a new level to attain. You might leave the Elementary level behind and move up to Beginner Novice. In jumping, you can simply compete at the next level of fence height.

Another way to gain experience is to upgrade your show circuit. Many competitors start out in shows put on by their local club. Once they are comfortable showing, they join a larger club that draws competitors from several towns. The next step is to go to a statewide show circuit. Many times these are sponsored by the state affiliate of a national organization, such as the American Quarter Horse Association or the Arabian Registry.

After a couple of years with the statewide organization, you can move on to the regional shows — New England–wide or a southern circuit. Then it's on to the nationals! For instance, if you show in AQHA-sanctioned events, your points are added up from August 1 through July 31. If you have placed in enough classes and accumulated enough points, the AQHA sends you a letter saying you have qualified for its huge World Show. Only a small percentage of those who qualify actually go, but if you feel you are ready for such a huge event, definitely go and experience it!

Changing Disciplines

Another way to shake up your show career is to try a new discipline. Maybe you are tired of pleasure classes and want to pop over a few fences. Dressage doesn't tend to attract a lot of youths, but maybe you feel it's time to abandon the hunter/jumper circuit and start the more exacting field of dressage. Or you could combine the two and try eventing, which consists of a day of dressage, a day of cross-country, and a day of stadium jumping. The best of all worlds!

Sometimes just putting on a new set of riding clothes can change the atmosphere enough. Take some

Play It Safe and Slow

Move up to a new horse or new level only when you are ready. Don't let anyone talk you into something you are uncomfortable with. The quaint saying that you will hear from lots of people is "This is supposed to be fun!" You should definitely have fun while showing, but it should also be challenging. However, don't make it so challenging that you start to dread shows because the jumps have become too high or your horse is too much for you.

When you change to a new horse, judge and trainer Lowell Murray advises that you move back a step for a show or two until you and your horse are comfortable together. The same goes for advancing to a higher-rated show circuit: Compete in an easier division at first.

It's hard, but you have to speak up and tell someone if you find that showing is no longer a pleasure. Talk with someone you trust about your concerns — your parents, your instructor, an older friend at the barn. That person may be

able to help you figure out why showing has become less enjoyable than it used to be. You can work together to find ways to make showing fun again.

If you want to reach the top level, you need to be willing to reach for it with all you have. Use your experience in smaller shows to tell you exactly where you need the most work — learn breathing techniques to relax, memorizing techniques to remember patterns. Having everything you need and being organized can be the most relaxing thing of all. And don't forget to use your fellow competitors to laugh with and help each other along.

lessons over the winter and ride English for a season. Unless your goal is to be an Olympian, in which case you need to stick to one discipline and become a master, there is no reason not to hop around a little. You'll learn something from every discipline and you'll meet lots of new, interesting people. Take the opportunity to ride different horses, as you will learn from each of them as well. If you own a horse, he would probably enjoy a change, too, and you might both return to your original discipline feeling relaxed and focused after a break.

A More Advanced Horse

No matter what your discipline, if you stick with showing, there will come a point when you will want to move up to a more advanced horse or a horse who has more potential to advance than the one you have. Maybe your current pony has taken you through the first two levels of dressage. Now it's time to move on and it may be time for a new horse. See chapter 4 for more information on purchasing or leasing a horse.

High Performance

If you want to go all the way to the top in riding, set your sights on the United States or Canadian Equestrian Team. These are the teams that compete at the Oympic Games, the World Cup, and other international events. The U.S. team competes in seven different disciplines: Show Jumping, Eventing, Driving, Dressage, Endurance Riding, Reining, and Vaulting.

Profile:
The North American Young Rider Championships

The NAYRC is an FEI (International Equestrian Federation or, in French, Fédération Equestre Internationale) competition and falls under all FEI rules and regulations. The Championships have been going on for more than a decade and young riders from all over North America, including Canada, and Mexico, gather in August to compete for team and individual titles.

The Championship has two basic divisions – Junior Riders ages 14 to 18 and Young Riders ages 16 to 21 – broken up according to zones. This is a high-level international competition and a goal worth aspiring to!

Reaching the level of participating in the NAYRC takes a monumental effort on your part. Some tips:

◆ Become a working student in the summer or on weekends at a barn where there are FEI-level horses. Even if you don't get to ride an FEI-level horse, you will learn a lot by watching.

◆ Learn how to balance school with your riding. The NAYRC emphasizes strong academics as well as good equitation, so you have to keep your grades up while training for high-level competition.

According to Dr. Lynn Budd, the Young Rider Coordinator for the U.S. Dressage Federation for Region 8 (New England and New York), "Kids who compete at this level are riding at least one horse every day. They usually need at least one year with a horse to develop the relationship they need with the horse to be successful at the FEI level."

What does competing at this level do for your future? According to Dr. Budd, the kids who make it onto the team are noticed by professionals in the field. They are competing under the same standards and some of the same judging panels as riders at the very top of the competition world. If you intend to continue on and compete at the highest levels, this exposure to the top equestrians in the world and learning how to deal with the pressure of high, tough competition is invaluable.

The rules are strict, so it pays to start studying them early! For the complete information packet for the North American Young Riders Championships, check out its Web site at www.youngriders.org or request one by mail to NAYRC, 17000 Wadsworth Road, Old Mill Creek, IL 60083; (847) 295-3285.

Show Story

Jill's horse, Fancy, is a 15-year-old gelding trained for English pleasure by his previous owner, who showed him in the B-rated pleasure show circuit for nearly ten years. Fancy was solid and experienced and helped Jill learn all about showing. As a team, they took home many ribbons in English pleasure. Last fall, Jill began jumping lessons and would like to compete in jumping this year. The big question: Is Fancy still the right horse for Jill?

The first year or two, Jill will probably show in low jumps, 2' to 2'6". Already a solid show horse, Fancy may take to jumping well and might actually enjoy doing something new. Before jumping him at any height, Jill should have her veterinarian check Fancy carefully. In addition to the usual checklist, the veterinarian will look for:

◆ arthritis and other problems that develop in the joints of older horses

◆ problems that might point to navicular disease

◆ respiratory health, keeping in mind that jumping takes more lung capacity than the rail work of English pleasure.

After Jill's first year or two of show jumping, though, she will probably be ready for another horse to take her further in her jumping career than Fancy can.

But Jill doesn't have to sell Fancy. She could lease him (usually free of charge) to a novice rider, and Fancy could start again as a show babysitter and teacher.

Meanwhile, she could find an experienced horse to free-lease from someone who is moving on to a higher level. Or she could ride more experienced horses in her lesson barn before buying one of her own.

Even if Jill does sell Fancy, she can sell him to a novice rider and be comfortable knowing her trusty mount went to someone who will really appreciate him.

Ask Yourself

Here are a few questions to ask yourself if you think it might be time to move to the next stage of showing:

Are you finding it harder to get motivated to practice for your shows?

_____

_____

Do you have the same level of enthusiasm you always had the morning of a show?

_____

_____

Does your horse seem bored with it all?

_____

_____

What does showing mean to you these days? Is it all about the ribbons? Or do you want it to be something more?

_____

_____

Are you willing to put in the time it will take to become competitive at the next level?

_____

_____

_____

Are you willing to not win for a few classes or even a few shows while you get your bearings in a higher-level circuit?

_____

_____

_____

Does your budget allow you the increased costs in tack, clothing, transportation, and entry fees that the higher-rated shows might require?

_____

_____

_____

Staying Organized

It's important to plan ahead so that you remember to take everything to the show. It's just as important to keep track of your stuff while you are there. Here are some checklists to help you stay organized. You can photocopy these lists and stick them in your tack trunk or hang them up in your trailer. Add your own ideas on the blank lines at the end.

Packing for Your Horse

- ❑ Water buckets
- ❑ Cooler blanket
- ❑ Fly sheet or mask in bug season
- ❑ Extra bell boots or other leg protection your horse normally wears
- ❑ Grooming kit in a special tote just for shows. This should include:
  - full set of brushes
  - mane and tail comb
  - hoof pick
  - several small towels
  - talcum powder or corn starch
  - hoof polish
  - Vaseline
  - braiding kit
- ❑ Medical kit just for shows. This should include:
  - Betadine
  - clotting powder such as WonderDust
  - Vetwrap
  - Banamine paste
  - Bute paste
  - gauze
  - electrolyte paste
  - white cotton facecloths or hand towels
  - thermometer

- small bucket reserved for washing wounds
- ❑ Enough grain, hay, and supplements for one day more than you need, especially if your horse eats grain that is hard to find or a special ration of any kind.
- ❑ Show halter
- ❑ Show leadrope
- ❑ Show bridle(s)
- ❑ Show saddle(s)
- ❑ Crop or dressage whip
- ❑ Clean saddle pad or blanket
- ❑ Extra set of stirrup pads
- ❑ Extra set of stirrup leathers
- ❑ General use halter and leadrope
- ❑ Longe whip
- ❑ Muck bucket or wheelbarrow
- ❑ Manure fork

What else?

- ❑ _____
- ❑ _____
- ❑ _____
- ❑ _____
- ❑ _____
- ❑ _____

Packing for Yourself

Use the extra lines at the end of this list to add your own "must-haves" for the show.

- ❏ Gloves
- ❏ Lapel pin
- ❏ Safety pins
- ❏ Hair care items (brush, hairpins, extra hairnets)
- ❏ Extra set of show clothes for all disciplines
- ❏ Riding boots
- ❏ Socks
- ❏ Mucking-around boots
- ❏ Raingear
- ❏ Helmet
- ❏ Jeans and t-shirt for non-showing wear
- ❏ Riding underwear (sports bra and/or seamless underpants)
- ❏ Schooling chaps (for warmup/practice time)
- ❏ Spurs

What else?

- ❏ _____
- ❏ _____
- ❏ _____

A Backpack of Extras

Along with all the stuff listed above, you will be happy if you pack the following as "extra supplies" in case they are needed:

- ❏ Fleece blanket (rolled up and tied)
- ❏ Granola bars and other snacks that keep well
- ❏ Bottled water
- ❏ Hair dryer
- ❏ Sunscreen
- ❏ Extra hair scrunches/clips/bobby pins/hairnet

- ❏ Warm hat
- ❏ Sun-shading hat
- ❏ Cooling bandana
- ❏ Small sewing kit
- ❏ Small first aid kit
- ❏ Extra socks
- ❏ Extra pair of bootlaces

What else?

- ❏ _____
- ❏ _____
- ❏ _____
- ❏ _____

Countdown to Show Time

Here are some checklists to help you plan and prepare for showing. As you gain experience, you might want to add your own tasks and reminders on the blank lines at the end of the lists.

Advance Preparations

❑ Research the upcoming show season and make a list of the shows you want to attend.

❑ Create a budget for the season.

❑ Finalize a realistic show schedule based on your budget, your transportation and horse availability, and other activities you and your family have planned during the season.

❑ Have your horse vaccinated, Coggins test taken, and health certificate applied for at least two weeks before your first show. Don't forget, your horse may need a couple days' break from schooling if he gets sore from vaccinations.

❑ Give your tack a thorough cleaning and make any necessary repairs.

❑ Wash your show sheets and blankets and make any necessary repairs.

❑ Replace any items that are worn or need upgrading (reins, blanket straps, etc.). Buy new equipment well ahead of time so you can break it in.

❑ If you have your own trailer, do a seasonal maintenance check: Examine the floor and tires (check air pressure!), have the wheel bearings repacked and the jack greased, replace the battery for the electric brakes if necessary. Make sure all the door latches are working and be sure wasps or ants have not taken up housekeeping in the trailer!

❑ Check the supplies that you keep in your trailer. Fill the first aid kits (both for humans and horses), restock your supply of shampoo and coat care products, fill up the bug spray containers.

❑ Check hay bags, hay nets, and buckets for wear and tear. Be sure you can find trailer ties if you use them.

What else?

❑ _____

❑ _____

❑ _____

❑ _____

❑ _____

❑ _____

❑ _____

The Night Before

❏ Make sure you have all your important documents in a folder in the car or truck cab. These should include: your horse's important papers — negative Coggins report, rabies certificate, and health certificate; any show paperwork you didn't send in ahead of time

❏ Load all your horse's equipment into the trailer

❏ Do the same with your own bags, whether they go in the trailer or the car. (Don't expect someone else to remember your stuff!)

❏ Check in with your traveling companions to make sure everyone knows the scheduled departure time and anything else you need to coordinate to ensure a smooth trip

❏ Fill hay nets and hay bags for the trip to the show

Show Morning

❏ Give your horse one last brushing and blanket him or bed his stall extra thick. Clean manure piles out as late as possible!

❏ Load your cooler of drinks and snacks

❏ Examine the hitch; make sure the ball is on securely if it's a tagalong

❏ Make sure the safety chains and safety brake line are attached

❏ Check that the trailer lights are working, especially the signals and brake lights.

❏ Once the horses are in, see that they are tied and content, with their hay bags in reach and not tangled in their halters.

❏ Check that all doors are tightly latched.

❏ Put extra lead ropes where they are easy to reach if something happens on the road and you have to unload the horses in a hurry.

❏ Before you drive away, check the horses and the trailer one more time, even if you did it right before you loaded them

❏ _____

❏ _____

❏ _____

❏ _____

❏ _____

After Each Show

Home again! Before the "show glow" wears off, do these tasks to make the next trip easier.

❏ Pick up trash and dispose of it properly

❏ Clean the floor of the trailer in the stall area

❏ Clean out hay nets and hay bags after the show and store for next time

❏ Vacuum and air out the trailer's tack area

❏ Restock the first aid kit (for both horses and humans) and other supplies

❏ Wash all your grooming brushes

❏ Make a list of anything that needs repair and let the appropriate person know

❏ _____

❏ _____

❏ _____

❏ _____

❏ _____

❏ _____

❏ _____

Show Diary

Use these pages to keep track of your horse-show adventures.

Date: _____

Name of Show: _____

Place: _____

Who I Went With: _____

Ribbons Won: _____

Class I Entered: _____

Horse I Rode: _____

What We Did Well: _____

_____

What Needs Improvement: _____

_____

_____

How We Placed: _____

_____

Class I Entered: _____

Horse I Rode: _____

What We Did Well: _____

_____

What Needs Improvement: _____

_____

_____

How We Placed: _____

_____

Class I Entered: _____

Horse I Rode: _____

What We Did Well: _____

_____

What Needs Improvement: _____

_____

_____

How We Placed: _____

_____

Ask Yourself

What was the best thing that happened during this show?

_____

_____

_____

Did the things I practiced help me in my classes?

_____

_____

_____

What should I focus on for improvement before the next show?

_____

_____

_____

Did my horse feel relaxed and act content about being there?

_____

_____

_____

Is this a show (club/grounds) I would like to come back to?

_____

_____

_____

Was I able to stick within my budget?

_____

_____

_____

What other classes do I want to try next time?

_____

_____

_____

_____

_____

_____

_____

Show Diary

Use these pages to keep track of your horse-show adventures.

Date: _____

Name of Show: _____

Place: _____

Who I Went With: _____

Ribbons Won: _____

Class I Entered: _____

Horse I Rode: _____

What We Did Well: _____

_____

What Needs Improvement: _____

_____

_____

How We Placed: _____

_____

Class I Entered: _____

Horse I Rode: _____

What We Did Well: _____

_____

What Needs Improvement: _____

_____

_____

How We Placed: _____

_____

Class I Entered: _____

Horse I Rode: _____

What We Did Well: _____

_____

What Needs Improvement: _____

_____

_____

How We Placed: _____

_____

Ask Yourself

What was the best thing that happened during this show?

_____

_____

_____

Did the things I practiced help me in my classes?

_____

_____

_____

What should I focus on for improvement before the next show?

_____

_____

_____

Did my horse feel relaxed and act content about being there?

_____

_____

_____

Is this a show (club/grounds) I would like to come back to?

_____

_____

_____

Was I able to stick within my budget?

_____

_____

_____

What other classes do I want to try next time?

_____

_____

_____

_____

_____

_____

Show Diary

Use these pages to keep track of your horse-show adventures.

Date: _____

Name of Show: _____

Place: _____

Who I Went With: _____

Ribbons Won: _____

Class I Entered: _____

Horse I Rode: _____

What We Did Well: _____

_____

What Needs Improvement: _____

_____

How We Placed: _____

_____

Class I Entered: _____

Horse I Rode: _____

What We Did Well: _____

_____

What Needs Improvement: _____

_____

How We Placed: _____

_____

Class I Entered: _____

Horse I Rode: _____

What We Did Well: _____

_____

What Needs Improvement: _____

_____

How We Placed: _____

_____

Ask Yourself

What was the best thing that happened during this show?

_____

_____

_____

Did the things I practiced help me in my classes?

_____

_____

_____

What should I focus on for improvement before the next show?

_____

_____

_____

Did my horse feel relaxed and act content about being there?

_____

_____

_____

Is this a show (club/grounds) I would like to come back to?

_____

_____

_____

Was I able to stick within my budget?

_____

_____

_____

What other classes do I want to try next time?

_____

_____

_____

_____

_____

Resources

American Hunter Jumper Association
P.O. Box 369
335 Lancaster Street
West Boylston, MA 01583
508-835-8813
www.ryegate.com/AHJF/ahjf.htm

American Miniature Horse Association
5601 South Interstate 35W
Alvarado, TX 76009
817-783-5600
www.amha.com

American Morgan Horse Association
122 Bostwick Rd.
P.O. Box 960
Shelburne, VT 05482
802-985-4944
www.morganhorse.com

American Paint Horse Association
P.O. Box 961023
Fort Worth, TX 76161
817-834-2742
www.apha.com

American Quarter Horse Association
P. O. Box 200
Amarillo, TX 79168
806-376-4811
www.aqha.com

Appaloosa Horse Club
2720 West Pullman Road
Moscow, ID 83843
208-882-5578
www.appaloosa.com

Arabian Horse Association
10805 East Bethany Drive
Aurora, CO 80014
303-696-4500
www.arabianhorses.org

Canadian Equestrian Federation
2460 Lancaster Road
Ottawa ON K1B 4S5
613-248-3433
www.equinecanada.com

Canadian Sport Horse Association
P.O. Box 1625
Holland Landing, ON L9N 1P2
905-830-9288
www.canadian-sport-horse.org

Intercollegiate Horse Show Association
www.insainc.com

National Barrel Horse Association
P.O. Box 1988
Augusta, GA 30903
706-722-7223
www.nhba.com

National Reining Horse Association
3000 NW 10th Street
Oklahoma City, OK 73107
1-405-946-7400
www.nhra.com

U.S. Eventing Association
525 Old Waterford Road NW
Leesburg, VA 20176
703-779-0440
www.eventingusa.org

U.S. Equestrian Federation
4047 Ironworks Parkway
Lexington KY 40511
859-258-2475
www.usef.com

U.S. Dressage Federation
220 Lexington Green Circle
Suite 510
Lexington KY 40503
859-971-2277
www.usdf.org

Interior Photography Credits

Index

Other Storey Titles You Will Enjoy

Dream Horses: A Poster Book, photographs by Bob Langrish. You will be enchanted by these 30 dreamlike scenes. The images have been manipulated so that each shot has a fantastical, even mythological quality. 64 pages. Paperback. ISBN 1-58017-574-0.

Games on Horseback, by Betty Bennett-Talbot and Steven Bennett. Improve your equestrian skills and have fun with friends using this collection of more than 50 safe, exciting, and challenging games for horse and rider. Paperback. ISBN 1-58017-134-6.

The Horse Breeds Poster Book, photographs by Bob Langrish. There are 30 full-color beauty shots in this book, each with an information-packed panel about the horse on the back of the poster. 64 pages. Paperback. ISBN 1-58017-507-4.

Horse Care for Kids, by Cherry Hill. An introduction to safe, responsible horsekeeping for young riders, including selecting a horse, feeding, grooming, and stable management. 128 pages. ISBN 1-58017-407-8 (paperback); ISBN 1-58017-476-0 (hardcover).

Horse Games & Puzzles for Kids, by Cindy A. Littlefield. Packed with 102 games and puzzles, including word-play games, picture puzzles, and brainteasers, this book will delight any horse-crazy kid. Paperback. ISBN 1-58017-538-4.

Riding for Kids, by Judy Richter. The perfect companion to lessons in the ring, with a focus on English riding skills and techniques. It is the complete learn-to-ride program every young equestrian will refer to again and again. 144 pages. ISBN 1-58017-510-4 (paperback); ISBN 1-58017-511-2 (hardcover).

Storey's Horse-Lover's Encyclopedia, edited by Deborah Burns. This hefty, fully illustrated, comprehensive A-to-Z compendium is an indispensable answer book addressing every question a reader may have about horses and horse care. 480 pages. ISBN 1-58017-317-9 (paperback); ISBN 1-58017-336-5 (hardcover).

Your Horse, by Judy Chapple. A thorough guide that is easy to comprehend, this book takes the mystery out of horse ownership, from getting your first horse to riding it. Paperback. ISBN 0-88266-353-4.

These books and other Storey books are available wherever books are sold, or directly from Storey Publishing, 210 MASS MoCA Way, North Adams, MA 01247 or by calling 1-800-441-5700. Visit us at www.storey.com.

Autographs